Letts EXPLORE

Prologue to the Canterbury Tales
GEOFFREY CHAUCER

Guide written by
Claire Wright

Series Editor: Stewart Martin

A *Letts* Literature Guide

Every effort has been made to trace copyright holders and to obtain their permission for the use of copyright material. The author and publishers will gladly receive information enabling them to rectify any reference or credit in subsequent editions.

First published 1995
Letts Educational
Aldine House
Aldine Place
London W12 8AW

Text © Claire Wright 1995

Typeset by Jordan Publishing Design

Text design Jonathan Barnard

Cover and text illustrations Hugh Marshall

Graphic illustration Hugh Marshall

Design © BPP (Letts Educational) Ltd

British Library Cataloguing in Publication Data
A CIP record for this book is available from the British Library

ISBN 1 85758 275 6

Printed and bound in Great Britain
by Ashford Colour Press Ltd, Gosport, Hants

Letts Educational is the trading name of BPP (Letts Educational) Ltd

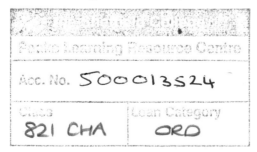

◼ Contents

'But nevertheless, while I have the chance,
Before I proceed with the story,
I think it appropriate
To tell you about the state
Of each of them, as it seemed to me,
And what sort of person they were,
And of what rank...'

MILITARY
Knight
Squire
Yeoman

CLERGY
Prioress
Monk
Friar

LAITY: UPPER MIDDLE CLASS
Merchant
Clerk
Sergeant-at-Law
Franklin
Guildsmen (and Cook)
Shipman
Physician
Wife of Bath

TWO GOOD MEN
Parson
Ploughman

ROYALTY/NOBILITY not represented as they would not have travelled in a mixed group.

THE ORDER OF THE PILGRIMS

LAITY: LOWER MIDDLE CLASS

Miller
Manciple
Reeve

CHURCH OFFICERS

Summoner
Pardoner

GEOFFREY CHAUCER

'And I had spoken with each
of them in such a way
That I was soon one of their
company...'

SERFS/PEASANTS not
represented as they would not
have been free to travel.

■ Who's who in
The General Prologue

The General Prologue is itself a 'Who's who' of the pilgrims who go on to tell *The Canterbury Tales*. In creating such a diverse portrait-gallery of characters, Chaucer found a brilliant new approach to the traditional collection of miscellaneous stories. He could add meaning and spice to the tales by having them told by appropriate – or surprising – characters, who also reveal more of themselves in their tales. The story-telling could be framed by the characters' banter, debates, personality clashes and general goings-on.

The vivid detail in the portraits gives an impression of realism, and suggests that Chaucer had specific living models for the characters. Yet the pilgrims are also representative types, who would have been familiar to Chaucer's audience from popular and literary tradition. Indeed, some characters are almost timeless: the pompous businessman and the poor student still seem familiar, 600 years later! Chaucer appears deliberately to have portrayed a cross-section of his society at the time *The General Prologue* was written (1387–92). Its diversity is professional, physical, social and moral: the poet John Dryden could only say of it, 'Here is God's plenty'.

It would be pointless to summarise Chaucer's 'Who's who'. The following notes explain the pilgrims' social roles and professions, which may be unfamiliar. They are grouped in the classes or 'estates' recognised by the medieval social order.

The military

The fourteenth century saw England and France engaged in the Hundred Years' War (1337–1453) and the knights of Christian Europe striving to conquer 'heathen' lands for the faith. **Knights** were the ruling class, supporting the king at home and abroad. There were also powerful religious/military orders of knights. Chivalry (the highly-developed system and moral code of knighthood) was declining by Chaucer's day, but his Knight illustrates its original ideals: courage, honour, service and humility. A typical career embraced pitched battles and chivalric tournaments, where knights fought and jousted under formal rules.

A **squire** was a well-born youth, trained to serve (and fight alongside) his knight, and aspiring to knighthood himself. Chaucer's Squire embodies the less warlike chivalric ideal: the code of courtly love, which emphasised joy, graceful accomplishments and dedicated service of the chosen mistress.

A **yeoman** was a knight's servant, ranking above a groom: only later was the term used for small landowners. Chaucer's yeoman carries a bow and arrows: archery (use of the bow) had an important role in medieval warfare.

The clergy

There were two kinds of clergy in the Catholic Church. The 'regular' clergy lived by a communal rule, as members of a religious order. Monks, nuns and friars lived in communities (monasteries or convents) where they devoted themselves (in theory) to prayer, study and work: they could also be priests, like Chaucer's Friar. The 'secular' clergy, like bishops and priests, lived in the outside world to minister to the people.

A **prioress** was the head of a priory or convent of nuns: a senior churchwoman.

Chaucer's **Monk** was an 'outrider', whose duty it was to ride out and inspect the estates of the monastery. The hunting monk, a lover of horses and dogs, was an established figure in popular tradition and a target of the reformers who had begun to attack clerical abuses.

Although regulars, **friars** were not bound to monastic life, but went into the world to preach the gospel, living off charity. By Chaucer's day, the mendicant (begging) orders had lost the pure motives of their founders, and the corrupt or 'venal' friar was another familiar target of satire and protest. Chaucer's Friar is a 'limiter', a friar who paid a rent to his convent to beg in an assigned district or 'limit'. He is also a 'licentiate', authorised by the Pope to take confessions and grant absolution – even in serious cases which priests had to refer to their bishops.

> It is worth understanding what the sacrament of **'penance'** involved. The church taught that sin would be punished: in hell (if the sinner died unrepentant) or in purgatory (where souls suffered to atone for their sins before going to heaven). Only God could forgive sin, but priests could grant absolution: remission, or release, from punishment. In order to be absolved or 'shriven', a sinner had to confess, repent and perform a penance (a token punishment, such as prayer or fasting) imposed by the priest.

A **parson** was a secular parish priest. He was responsible for the sacraments, preaching and (ideally) 'pastoral' care. His parishioners paid a tithe (one tenth of their income) to support him. He could report non-payers to the bishop for excommunication (exclusion from the Church). Chaucer's Parson avoids this and other abuses of clerical power which were attacked by the reformers.

Summoners were church officers who called offenders to appear before ecclesiastical courts, presided over by an archdeacon (ranking below a bishop). The courts dealt with offences such as witholding of tithes, perjury, heresy and sexual immorality. They could impose fines, backed by the threat of excommunication, which in turn could lead to imprisonment: there was plenty of scope for bribery and extortion, for which summoners were legendary.

Pardoners were sellers of papal indulgences or 'pardons': certificates from the pope, giving remission from penance – or time in purgatory – for payment to a church charity. Originally, this was a 'tax on sin' which benefited the needy, but by Chaucer's time, many supposed pardoners were unauthorised and their papers false: they kept the money. The Church itself condemned these abuses. Chaucer's Pardoner has another fraudulent business on the side, selling fake relics (body parts or belongings of a saint) which were venerated as holy in the churches.

The bourgeoisie

In the old feudal system, no 'middle class' existed: there were ruling landowners, clergy and farm labourers. But by Chaucer's day, trade and commerce were booming, creating a rapidly-expanding class of prosperous and educated craftsmen, traders and professionals. This is reflected in the diversity of Chaucer's group and the vaguer sense of their rank order. Chaucer satirises their frankly acquisitive values. The financially independent but socially aspiring upper-middle class and the grasping lower-middle class who serve them are exposed by the contrast with unworldly individuals like the Clerk and Ploughman.

Merchants were a newly rich and powerful class. Chaucer's Merchant typically deals in imports and exports, with hints of (illegal) currency exchange and money-lending.

Sergeants-at-Law were the king's legal servants, selected from the most eminent senior barristers: in Chaucer's day, there were only about twenty. They supplied the regular judges of the king's courts, and also circuit judges for assizes (sessions of county courts).

The term **'clerk'** applied to a man in holy orders, as well as to an ecclesiastical student. Chaucer's Clerk has 'not yet' got a church living, and is pursuing further studies, perhaps for a Master's degree. The threadbare, borrowing student was a familiar figure in Chaucer's England – some things do not change!

Franklins were landholders of free (but not noble) birth. There is some debate as to whether they were considered 'gentry' to rank alongside knights, esquires and sergeants-at-law. Chaucer's Franklin is wealthy, and eminent enough to have been knight of the shire (member of parliament) and sheriff, the king's administrative officer in a county.

The **guilds** were originally trade or craft fraternities, but religious and social guilds also developed as the focus of urban middle class social life. 'Aldermen' were both guild officers and municipal magistrates: prominent citizens. The aspirations of Chaucer's group extend to having their own **Cook** with them.

The **Shipman** is not just a sailor but a master of his ship, engaged by merchants to carry imported goods.

Medieval **physicians** used not only physic (medicinal treatments) and surgery, but also astrology and 'natural' (not 'black') magic, such as talismans and wax images: Chaucer's Physician is not to be considered a quack. Chaucer notes that doctors had done well out of the Black Death – the plagues of 1349 and the 1360s, which wiped out a third of the population in England and almost caused the collapse of the feudal economy.

The **Wife of Bath** is able to travel, as a financially independent woman, thanks to her trade in cloth – and her ex-husbands. The vain, domineering, lustful wife was a stereotype of anti-feminist satire.

Chaucer's **Ploughman** is not the base rustic of contemporary satire, nor a militant fresh from the 1381 Peasants' Revolt. He is not a serf, but a freeman, apparently a small tenant farmer.

Millers ran the corn-mills. They had a monopoly on grinding corn (to meal or flour) for the farmers in their district, and they notoriously exploited it by under-measuring and over-charging.

A **manciple** was a comparatively obscure servant, who purchased provisions for a college or an inn of court (society of lawyers), such as the Inner or Middle Temple in London.

A **reeve** was an estate manager. Normally, the hierarchy ran (from the top down): lord of the manor, steward, bailiff, provost and reeve. However, Chaucer's Reeve deals directly with his lord, rules bailiffs and accumulates property: his rôle approaches that of a steward.

The Host

The Host

The pilgrims' Host is the innkeeper at 'The Tabard'. The Cook later calls him Harry Bailly. (A man of that name is registered as an innkeeper in Southwark in 1380, and as a public servant in the area between 1376 and 1394: a plausible model for Chaucer's Host.)

As master of ceremonies and instigator of the tale-telling game, the Host plays an important rôle in the narrative and in the structure of *The Canterbury Tales* as a whole. In *The General Prologue* he unites the pilgrims as a band, establishes the rules of the contest and imposes his own personality as leader: jolly, shrewd, flattering and bullying by turns. Later, he holds together the framework of the tales by directing the speakers, commenting approvingly or rudely on the tales and controlling the unruly pilgrims (albeit in a rather unruly fashion!) Apart from Chaucer's occasional comments as narrator, the Host is the only consistent voice between the Tales: a unifying element amid the diverse styles and subjects.

Chaucer

Chaucer

Chaucer presents himself as a character in *The Canterbury Tales*: he joins the pilgrims, sociably, at 'The Tabard'. He is also the self-conscious narrator of the poem, who apologises to the reader for his shortcomings.

As pilgrim-narrator, Chaucer is impressed by the wealth, professional prowess and social standing of his companions. He takes them very much at face value, by appearances and their own estimation of themselves. (They are all apparently unequalled at what they do.) He seems unaware that his descriptions of dress, behaviour and appearance can conceal – or reveal – deeper aspects of their personalities. The pilgrim-narrator uses words like 'good', 'worthy' and 'noble' with an apparent lack of discrimination. At the same time, he rather prides himself on being a man of the world, at home in mixed company, able to converse on trade, law and medicine, broad-minded, but wise to society's rascals.

Beneath all this, however, we are aware of Chaucer the poet: not so impressionable, indiscriminate or guileless as his narrator persona. His viewpoint is subtly revealed: in significant details of face, manner and dress; in ambiguous or double-edged words; in the use of contrasts and echoes to point to moral differences or similarities between characters. The poet's voice is full of irony, at the expense of his characters (and of his innocent alter ego, the pilgrim-narrator, who sees nothing of what the real Chaucer sees).

When the narrator says 'My wit is short, you may well understand', it is not false modesty on Chaucer's part, but a joke at his own expense. The joke gets even richer in the Tales. The Sergeant-at-Law disparages Chaucer's poetry and Chaucer's tale of Sir Thopas (a parody of conventional versifying) is cut short by an exasperated Host, who thinks his tedious doggerel 'not worth a turd'. Chaucer then launches into the tale of Melibeus in *prose*!

Chaucer was a very learned and well-read man for his time, and also widely experienced in war and diplomacy, court and trade. (There is a brief account of his life on page 16 of this guide.) His viewpoint is at once comic and profound, moral and humane.

■ Themes and images in
The General Prologue

The Church

The Church

Chaucer's time was a critical period for the Catholic Church, which for centuries had held absolute religious and political power. In Europe, 1378 saw the start of the Great Schism, with rival popes in Rome and Avignon. In England, the reformer John Wycliffe (*c.* 1328-84) and his followers the Lollards attacked the wealth of the clergy, challenged the Church's authority in worldly affairs and even rejected Church doctrines (such as penances and absolution). They translated Scripture into English (from Latin) for the first time.

Chaucer shows cautious sympathy for some of these views. He portrays a Church which has 'sold out' to worldly values and aspirations: in the lax discipline and worldly conduct of his Prioress, Monk and Friar; in his deeper indignation at the thought of mercenary absentee priests who leave their flocks for the easy life in London. His portraits of the clergy also highlight the worst contemporary abuses within the Church: exploitation of power, hypocrisy and corruption. It would be a mistake to see Chaucer as anti-clerical, however: his portrait of the Parson is glowing in its commendation of what a Christian minister should and could be.

It is difficult for us today to understand the Church's hold over lives and minds in Chaucer's time. Christian theology and tradition were the basis of all social arrangements. Every aspect of study was interpreted in the light of beliefs about God, man and the universe, sin and salvation. Despite the shortcomings of individuals and institutions, Christianity provided a set of social, cultural and religious values which were more or less consistent, understood and shared by everyone. No alternative secular system had yet emerged to fragment this sense of certainty and belonging.

Chaucer's understanding of humanity (and his delight in it) must be seen in the context of this view. His portraits of the pilgrims are vivid and realistic, but they have a clear moral and spiritual dimension. We may call this 'Christian humanism': a viewpoint centred on both God and man.

Virtue

Virtue

Virtues, in Chaucer's time, were defined by two prevailing systems of thought: Christianity and chivalry.

Christian virtues include the four 'cardinal' virtues, thought to be the most important: prudence (good judgement), justice (fairness), fortitude (courage and strength of character) and temperance (moderation). Look for corresponding qualities in Chaucer's characters. The Knight possesses all of them, as does the Parson. Chaucer also uses the terms ironically: the Physician practices self-control in his diet, but it is hinted that this may be linked to meanness; several of the characters are said to be prudent, but more in the sense of shrewd (and sharp) in their business practices.

In addition, there were three 'theological' virtues of faith, hope and charity (love of one's fellow human beings): the greatest of these, according to Scripture, was charity. Note that 'charity' is a specific attribute of the Ploughman — and that, again, it is used in a rather subversive way in the portrait of the Wife of Bath, who swiftly ran out of 'charity' if she was not given precedence in church.

Chivalric virtues included courtesy (or good manners), humility, valour, honourable dealing (keeping one's word) and service (not for money, but for God, King and one's Mistress). The Knight and Squire are the ideals here.

You may identify other moral qualities Chaucer admired: he mentions honesty, compassion and tolerance. Words like 'noble', 'gentil', 'good' and 'worthy' abound in his descriptions, and you should try to be clear in your own mind what moral value they actually imply in each case.

Vice

Vice

Sin and salvation were the central issues of medieval thought. To Chaucer and his contemporaries, the Seven Deadly Sins were not only religious and cultural symbols: they were spiritual realities which were actually 'deadly' to the soul. The Seven Deadly Sins were pride, envy, anger, sloth (laziness), avarice (greed), gluttony and lechery (lust).

Many of Chaucer's Tales have explicit or underlying moral themes: the Pardoner's Tale, for example, is a sermon 'exemplum' (or illustration) of the effects of the sin of avarice.

In *The General Prologue*, the moral framework of the Tales is not yet fully established, but the portraits indicate that *cupiditas* or avarice, in particular, is going to be a major theme. Avarice is seen in dishonest profit-seeking and exploitation, but also in meanness or miserliness, and in ostentatious displays of wealth: all show a love of money. Most of Chaucer's middle-class pilgrims (with the notable exception of the Clerk and the Ploughman) are motivated by it. However, Chaucer saves his indignation for the corrupt and greedy churchmen, sinking to a contemptible low in the person of the Pardoner.

'Allegory' (where characters and events are used as metaphors for what happens in the moral or spiritual sphere) was a common literary device of Chaucer's time. His characters are too rounded to be mere personifications of the Seven Deadly Sins, but look out for aspects of the Sins in each of them: the Merchant's pride, the Franklin's gluttony, the Miller's anger, and more widespread lustfulness and avarice. Consider how Chaucer regards them: whether with indulgence, amusement, disgust or indignation.

Food and drink

The topic of food and drink is one of the motifs by which Chaucer describes and compares his pilgrims. It appears in different aspects: the Prioress's fastidious table manners; the Monk's love of roast swan (not standard monastic fare!); the Franklin's Epicurean table; the rather basic repertoire of

Food and drink the pretentious Guildsmen's Cook; the Physician's frugal diet; the Manciple's 'resourceful' catering; the Summoner's unhealthy love of pungent food and strong wine; the Host's hospitality; and finally the meal put up as prize for the tale-telling contest.

The pilgrims' eating and drinking habits, described at face value by Chaucer the innocent pilgrim, are used by Chaucer the ironic poet to give an insight into their temperaments.

Pilgrimage

Pilgrimages occupied a central place in medieval life. A pilgrimage, as an act of piety and sacrifice, might be imposed as a penance for one's sins; it might be undertaken to give thanks to God for blessings received; a person might vow to go on a pilgrimage if spared from sickness or danger.

Pilgrimage Others went simply for the adventure of travel (with spiritual 'Brownie points' thrown in!), for social companionship, or to make money along the way from gullible fellow pilgrims. The most frequently visited shrines in England were the shrine of Our Lady of Walsingham in Norfolk and the shrine of St Thomas Becket in Canterbury. Well-established routes developed, with places of rest and hospitality along the way. Chaucer himself went on a pilgrimage to Canterbury in 1387.

The pilgrimage framework offered Chaucer a way of bringing together a very diverse group of people to tell the Tales: pious pilgrims and charlatans; a high-ranking knight and a lowly ploughman. Pilgrimages were great social levellers: despite the fixed, and accepted, social hierarchy of the time, it was natural for different classes to mix freely. As John Wain, the poet and critic, comments: 'In that feudal world which had never heard of "equality", it was easier for a poor man to be close to an aristocrat, to eat the same food, to endure the same mud and weather, and to pray at the same shrine, than it has ever been in our chain-store democracy.'

The pilgrimage also gave Chaucer an image of life itself, which overarches the diversity of the Tales, and draws out the serious moral undercurrents of the comedy. At the end of the Tales, the Parson recalls the pilgrims' thoughts to God and the way of salvation: 'the way... of that perfect and glorious pilgrimage that is called the heavenly Jerusalem'.

Structure and sources of
The Canterbury Tales

Chaucer's original conception required 30 pilgrims to tell 4 stories each: that's 120 stories – not including linking passages, the Host's judgement of the winner and so on. Only nine 'fragments', in doubtful order, were completed. At the end, the Host says his 'plan is almost fulfilled', when one tale has been heard from each rank among them: Chaucer may have revised his original intentions, or simply run out of time. Some pilgrims (such as the Guildsmen) do not have a tale, some tales are incomplete (such as the Cook's) and others are told by people (such as the Canon's Yeoman) who do not appear in the Prologue. Even so, the work is remarkable for its range and variety.

The collection, or compendium, of stories was a familiar tradition in the Middle Ages. Many of the collections in use before Chaucer were simply random accumulations, or else books of *exempla* (illustrative stories) for use in preaching and moral instruction. The first notable example of a writer containing and unifying such a collection is the *Decameron* by the Italian Boccaccio: a group of noble Florentines take refuge in a castle from the plague and amuse themselves by telling stories. John Gower, a friend of Chaucer's, drew together a collection of stories within an allegorical framework in his *Confessio Amantis*: the stories are told as *exempla* by a priest, Genius, as he leads Amans (The Lover) through his confession. In about 1374, Giovanni Sercambi used the setting of a pilgrimage in his *Novelle*, although all the stories are told by the pilgrim-author.

Having collected a stock of stories through his travels and wide reading in French and Italian literature, Chaucer wanted a linking device that would use them to best advantage. The tale-telling contest, in the course of a pilgrimage, was a unique idea.

The Canterbury Tales embrace a wide variety of literary forms, as you might expect from the pilgrims: the high romance of courtly love (the Knight's Tale); pious legends about the lives of saints (the Prioress) and virtuous women (the Sergeant-at-Law, the Clerk); fairy-tale romances (the Wife of Bath); racy farces or *fabliaux* (the Miller, Reeve, Shipman, Merchant, Summoner); beast fable (the Nun's Priest); *exemplum* (the Pardoner) and prose sermon (the Parson). The *fabliaux* tellers all incorporate each other in their scurrilous tales: the tellers themselves are typical *fabliaux* figures, lecherous and deceitful. This creates an amusing cross-current of grudges and point-scoring between the tales.

Chaucer's poetry

In an age when literacy and book-owning were still comparatively rare, reading was not a solitary or silent pursuit, as it tends to be today. It was a 'performance' art. Even solitary readers tended to read aloud, or at least murmur the words. People were used to the oral delivery of sermons, tales and songs, even the 'news': they were skilled listeners.

Medieval poetry is meant to be read aloud, and its effects are specifically intended for the ear. Be alert to the following features of Chaucer's verse, which arise directly from the oral tradition:

Rhyme: English poetry up to the thirteenth century did not rhyme: it relied for its formal effects on rhythmic alliteration. This remained the style in Northern England, as in Langland's allegorical poem, *Piers Plowman*. ('Preyers of a parfit man and penaunce discret/Is the levest Labour that our Lord pleseth.') In the South, influenced by French literary trends, people's ears were charmed by rhyme. It not only sounded musical and clever, it provided a formal pattern which aided the reciter's memory and the listener's comprehension. Rhyme was an important and subtle technique, used for expressive effects, puns and the ironic linking of incongruous words, like 'cloister' and 'oyster'.

Rythm: Many words in Middle English had a final 'e' which was pronounced only slightly. This created the effect of a bright, flowing rhythm, within a basic five-beat line (or pentameter), which Chaucer in any case used with unusual freedom and variety. The movement and lightness of his verse is almost impossible to reproduce in translation. Try saying the following line, marked (') where the stress falls, and (ë) for the light final syllable: 'And smálë fówlës máken mélodíë'.

Redundancy: Oral communication requires more strictly superfluous elements than written communication. Think about the fillers you use when talking to someone: stalling phrases like 'What I mean to say is', markers like 'you know...' and so on. Medieval poetry contains formal patterned effects, similarly designed to help the reciter and listener: rhymes, oaths, clichés, repetitions, parallel phrases. They do not necessarily have a specific dramatic or expressive role. Chaucer's narrative verse style is comparatively loose and uneconomical: what has been called 'an easy long-distance style'.

Consider how Chaucer addresses us directly in *The General Prologue*. Do you feel that his tone is that of a writer to a solitary reader – or a speaker to an audience of listeners?

■ Geoffrey Chaucer

Geoffrey Chaucer was born in about 1343, in the reign of Edward III – just after the beginning of the Hundred Years' War with France, and just before the Black Death (1349) which killed a third of the population of England. Chaucer's father was a London wine merchant, one of the emerging prosperous upper-middle class of the time. The young Geoffrey served as a page in the household of King Edward's son Prince Lionel and fought in France in 1359-60. Later, he also gained an important patron in John of Gaunt, another of Edward's sons: his wife Philippa was the sister of Katherine Swynford – John's mistress and later wife.

Chaucer travelled 'on the king's business' to Flanders and France, and later to Italy in 1372 and 1378. Here he become acquainted with the work of Dante, Petrarch and Boccaccio, as well as seeing the emerging great cities of Milan, Florence and Pisa. Having already absorbed the fashionable French style of rhyming pentameter, Chaucer now assimilated Italian influences and sources. He was undoubtedly an unusually learned man for his time: he read and spoke Latin, French and Italian and had a wide range of interests in science, philosophy and theology – as we can see from *The General Prologue*.

Between 1374 and 1386, Chaucer held the important post of Controller of Customs and Subsidies on Wools, Skins and Hides in the Port of London: duties on wool were a main source of Crown revenue. It was a turbulent period. The war and crusades dragged on. Richard II came to the throne in 1377. Social unrest had been growing since the second outbreak of the plague in the 1360s: in 1381, the Peasants' Revolt, led by Wat Tyler, almost took London – sacking John of Gaunt's palace in the process. Meanwhile, the Church was in crisis: the Great Schism of 1378 saw rival popes in Avignon and Rome, while Wycliffe and his followers the Lollards campaigned for reform (supported by John of Gaunt).

In 1386, Chaucer became a Justice of the Peace and Knight of the Shire (Member of Parliament) for Kent. At about the same time, he began to write *The Canterbury Tales*. He was hardly a reclusive writer, however. In 1389, he was appointed Clerk of the King's Works, in charge of the maintenance of royal residences, including Westminster Palace and The Tower. In 1391, he 'retired' to the less strenuous post of Deputy Forester of royal forests in Somerset. He was confirmed in the appointment by Henry IV, John of Gaunt's son, who deposed Richard II in 1399.

Chaucer died in 1400. You can still see his tomb today, in Westminster Abbey in London.

Our translation

We have not attempted to reflect Chaucer's poetic art, or the unique tone and flavour of his writing: these aspects are discussed in the commentary. The line breaks and numbers are meant only to help you follow the translation beside the original text. Our translation is offered as an aid to understanding the original work; it should not be read in isolation. Read it side by side with the original text for the full 'flavour' of Chaucer's style.

Our translation keeps as closely as possible to the order and literal meaning of Chaucer's words, so that you can make steady and accurate progress through the original (without footnotes!) You may like to think how you would rework our translation into more natural modern English. For example, **'people of various types'** (line 25) could be translated as 'a mixed bunch' for a more vivid – and quite Chaucerian – feel.

Words separated by an oblique – like **drought/dryness** in line 2 – are used where the Chaucerian word (droghte) has a recognisable modern equivalent which is an acceptable translation, but for which there is a more contemporary or accurate alternative. We give the equivalent word, (a) as a guide to where you are in the original, and (b) to show that Chaucer's language is not quite as 'foreign' as you might have feared!

Square brackets – like **[soote]** in line 1 – pinpoint the original word, where it may not be immediately recognisable in translation. In some cases, they also highlight words whose meaning has changed: **shoots [croppes]** in line 7 indicates that 'croppes' is not the recognisable word 'crops' (like wheat), but plant shoots in general. You may come across some alternative spellings, depending on which edition of Chaucer you are using.

Ordinary brackets – like **(knights of)** in line 53 – are used to insert words which do not appear in the text itself, but which are understood or implied from the context and grammatical form of the original phrase. They are also used to insert explanations, expansions and alternative translations where they might convey the meaning more fully.

■ Translation and commentary

Introduction (Lines 1–18)

1   When April with its sweet [soote] showers
Has pierced to the root the drought/dryness of March
And bathed every vein/sap-vessel in that liquor/moisture
By whose power [vertu] the flower is engendered/brought forth;
5   When Zephyr too [eek] with his sweet breath
Has inspired/quickened in every wood [holt] and heath
The tender shoots [croppes], and the young sun
Has run his half-course in the sign of the Ram,
And small birds [foweles] make melody –
10   Those that sleep all night with an eye open
(So nature pricks/spurs their hearts [corages]);
Then folk/people long to go on pilgrimages,
And palmers to visit strange/foreign shores,
To distant shrines [ferne halwes], known in sundry/different lands;
15   And especially, from every shire's end
Of England, they travel [wende] to Canterbury,
To seek out the holy blessed [blisful] martyr
Who helped them when they were sick.

Chaucer at 'The Tabard' (Lines 19–42)

It so happened that one day, at that time of year,
20   As I lay/lodged at 'The Tabard' in Southwark,
Ready to go on my pilgrimage
To Canterbury, with a most devout heart [corage],
At night there arrived at that hostelry
A full twenty-nine people in a company/group,
25   Of sundry/various types, fallen by chance [aventure]
Into fellowship/companionship, and they were all pilgrims
Who intended to [wolden] ride towards Canterbury.
The chambers/rooms and stables were spacious [wyde]
And we were entertained most excellently [esed atte beste].
30   And, in short, when the sun had gone to rest (ie set),
I had spoken with each one of them in such a way
That I was one of their fellowship/group immediately [anon],
And promised [made forward] to rise early,
To set off for where/the journey I am telling you about.
35   But nevertheless, while I have time and opportunity [space],
Before I proceed [ferther…pace] with this story,
I think it reasonable/appropriate
To tell you about the condition/state
Of each of them, as it seemed/appeared to me,
40   And what sort of person they were, and of what rank [degree],
And also what dress [array] they wore;
And therefore [than] I will begin with a Knight.

Introduction

Chaucer's description of Spring is more 'poetic' than the portraits and narrative to follow. (**Zephyr**, for example, is the classical god of the west wind.) But he links the conventional opening to the pilgrimage: nature's restlessness includes people, and Spring was the first season for travel after the short days and muddy roads of winter.

Chaucer often describes times and dates using astronomy. The **sun** was 'young' because it was early in the zodiacal year, which began with the sign of Aries (the **ram**). The sun entered Aries on March 12th for a month-long course. The Sergeant-at-Law later says the date is April 18th, so the sun has already run the *second* half of that course (and is now in Taurus).

Pilgrimage

Palmers were pilgrims to Jerusalem, who wore palms as a token. (On centres and motives for pilgrimage, see our note in the *Themes and images* section.)

The **holy blessed martyr** was Thomas Becket, a military commander and Lord Chancellor of England who became a well-loved Archbishop of Canterbury. He came into conflict with King Henry II and in 1170 was murdered in the cathedral by some of Henry's knights. Thomas was later canonised, but Canterbury was already a place of pilgrimage for the common people. St Thomas was associated with healing miracles.

> While exploring the background of Chaucer's words, don't neglect his skilled use of the words themselves. For example, 'inspired' (line 6) literally means 'breathed (life) into', enriching the Zephyr image. 'Seek' and 'sick' (lines 17–18) form a classic punning rhyme, much valued in medieval verse.

Chaucer at 'The Tabard'

About to set off for Canterbury, Chaucer meets a band of fellow pilgrims.

Southwark, in south London, was a common starting point, and there was

Chaucer

a Tabard Inn there. It is thought Chaucer himself made a pilgrimage when his wife was ill in 1387: possibly also the time he started *The General Prologue*. Here we meet **Chaucer the pilgrim**. He is pious, but appreciative of comfort and entertainment. He is sociable and swiftly accepted by all the pilgrims. (Their portraits are supposedly based on his conversations with them during that one evening!)

Chaucer tells his audience that he is going to describe the nature, dress, type and rank of his pilgrims. Consider, as you read their portraits, how he uses these categories of information. **Rank** was central to medieval society. Chaucer signals his intention to follow rank order, by starting with the Knight – departures from the 'proper' order will be significant.

The Knight (Lines 43–78)

A Knight there was, a worthy/distinguished man,
Who, from the time when he first began
45 To ride out/go campaigning, had loved chivalry,
Loyalty [trouthe] and honour, generosity [fredom] and courtesy.
He distinguished himself in his lord's/king's war,
And moreover [thereto] he had campaigned, no man further,
Both in Christendom and in heathen lands,
50 And was always honoured for his valour and virtue [worthynesse].
He was at Alexandria (in Egypt) when it was won/taken.
Very often he sat in the place of honour [hadde the bord bigonne]
Above (knights of) all nations in Prussia;
He had fought in raids [reysed] in Lithuania, and in Russia –
55 No Christian man oftener, of his rank.
In Granada (in Moorish Spain), he had been at the siege
Of Algeciras, and had ridden/fought in Benmarin (in Morocco).
He was at Ayas (in Armenia) and at Attalia (in Turkey),
When they were won/taken; and in the Mediterranean [Grete See]
60 He had been in many a noble armada/armed expedition.
He had been in fifteen mortal/pitched battles
And fought for our faith at Tramissene (Tlemçen, in Algeria)
In the (tournament) lists three times, and always slain his foe.
This same [ilke] worthy/distinguished knight had also been
65 With the lord/king of Palathia (Balat)
Against another heathen in Turkey.
And always he had an outstanding reputation [sovereign prys];
And although he was valourous [worthy], he was prudent [wys]
And in his bearing [port] as meek/modest as a maid.
70 He had never yet spoken a discourteous word [vileynye]
In all his life to any manner/kind of man.
He was a true [verray], perfect/complete, noble [gentle] knight.
But, to tell you of his array/equipment,
His horses were good, but he was not gaily/showily dressed [gay].
75 He wore a tunic [gypon] of fustian
All spotted (with rust) by his hauberk/coat of mail [habergeon],
For he was recently [late] returned from his voyage/travels
And was making his pilgrimage.

The Knight

The Knight comes first – not only in rank, as one of the ruling class of

The military

medieval Europe, but for the respect he personally commands. He embodies the ideals of courtly society, whose higher levels (royalty and nobility) could not be included in the pilgrim band. In particular, he is summed up as the 'true, complete, noble knight' (line 72). It has been suggested that Chaucer is satirising a corrupt contemporary chivalry by describing such a paragon of virtue, but do you think his tone in the text actually supports that view?

There are good poetic reasons for making the Knight an ideal figure. He sets a standard against which all the other pilgrims will be measured. He is described as 'worthy' (his key word, repeated several times), 'verray' 'perfect', 'gentle', 'wys'. Here, Chaucer uses these words sincerely and in their highest moral sense: the same words will be used for other pilgrims, but ironically, or in different senses. Similarly, the Knight is described in

Chaucer

superlatives (lines 48, 55, 67): other pilgrims are also said to be the epitome of their kind, but we may question the truth of the assertion – or whether it is a compliment! Although Chaucer the pilgrim is impressed by most of his fellows, Chaucer the poet reserves his unqualified approval for very few characters: the Knight is one of them. (He later tells one of the best tales, the model of a high courtly romance.)

Virtue

The Knight is described in terms of virtue and action rather than physical appearance. Line 46 epitomises the **chivalric ideal**: loyal service, honour (keeping one's word), generosity (neither miserliness nor extravagance) and courteous behaviour. Lines 68ff add the combination of courage and prudence (wise judgement) and humility. These qualities are, pointedly, not only chivalric but Christian: the 'cardinal' virtues of justice, temperance, prudence and fortitude.

The Knight's career included **'his lord's war'** (with France), but he mainly fought for the Christian faith. He took part in the campaigns in Moorish Spain and North Africa in 1343-44. He must have served under the brilliant Pierre de Lusignan (who took Attalia in 1361, Alexandria in 1365 and Ayas in 1367): the 'heathen' king of Palathia was bound in treaty to Pierre. He seems to have fought with the Teutonic Order of Knights in Lithuania and Russia. Lithuania turned Christian in 1386, so if our scene is set in April 1387, we can imagine the Knight just returned (line 77) and making a pilgrimage to give thanks for success and safe return.

Chaucer describes the Knight's clothes almost as an afterthought, but establishes his method of hinting at character by outward appearance. The Knight's clothes were not gay (bright, or showy), and bore the marks of recent fighting: he is obviously not worldly, vain or proud.

The Squire (Lines 79–100)

With him there was his son, a young Squire,
80 A lover and a vigorous [lusty] candidate for knighthood [bacheler]
With locks as curly as if they had been pressed/set (in curling tongs).
He was twenty years of age, I guess.
In stature he was of medium height [evene lengthe],
And wonderfully active (or agile) [delyvere] and strong.
85 And at one time he had taken part in cavalry raids [chyvachie]
In Flanders, Artois and Picardy,
And bore/conducted himself well, in such a brief opportunity [space],
Hoping to stand in/win his lady's grace/favour.
He was embroidered like a meadow
90 Full of fresh (or bright) flowers, white and red.
He was singing or fluting (possibly whistling) all day;
He was as fresh (or bright) as the month of May.
His gown was short, with long, wide sleeves.
He could sit a horse well, and ride expertly [faire].
95 He could make up songs and compose good lyrics [wel endite]
Joust and also dance, and draw [purtraye] and write well.
He loved so hotly/passionately, that by night
He slept no more than a nightingale does.
He was courteous, humble and willing to serve [servysable],
100 And carved (the meat) before/in front of his father at the table.

The Yeoman (Lines 101–117)

He (the Knight) had a Yeoman, and no other [namo] servants
On that occasion, for that is how it pleased [liste] him to travel,
And he was clad in a coat and hood of green.
A sheaf of peacock (feathered) arrows, bright and keen/sharp,
105 He bore under/hung from his belt most handily [thriftily],
(He knew well how to dress/look after his tackle/gear as a yeoman should:
[yemanly]
His arrows did not droop in flight because of poor feathering)
And in his hand he bore/carried a mighty bow.
He had a 'nut' head (close-cropped hair), with a brown face.
110 He was expert in all the practice [usage] of woodcraft.
On his arm he bore a gay/flashy arm-guard [bracer],
And by his side a sword and buckler/shield,
And on the other side a bright [gay] dagger
Well mounted and sharp as a spearpoint;
115 On his breast, a St Christopher (medal) of shiny/bright silver.
He carried a horn, the baldric/belt was of green;
He was a forester, truly [soothly], I would guess.

The Squire

The military

Chaucer himself trained as a page, and fought (in 1369) in Artois and Picardy, lands claimed by England in the war with France.

The Squire embodies another ideal of courtly society: the well-born young lover. He has all the right qualities and accomplishments, both manly (jousting and riding) and courtly (dancing, singing, drawing and writing). In these aspects, he too is set up as a standard against which other pilgrims will be measured. Note that in the code of courtly love, sexual prowess was part of the ideal: we are not meant to group the Squire with the 'lecherous' characters who are later said to love 'hotly'.

Virtue

Nor are we meant to think less of him for his show of valour in the wars 'to win his lady's favour': although his motives are contrasted with the Knight's, he simply embodies the romantic (rather than warlike) virtues of chivalry. He shares many of his father's qualities: courtesy, humility, willingness to serve. Nevertheless, Chaucer establishes another of the poetic methods that will be used, to less innocent effect, later on: contrast. Note the difference between the Knight's dress and his son's.

> The Squire's key word is 'fresh', which sums up the portrait's innocent charm and brightness. Chaucer jokes indulgently about his youthful passion: note the cheerful puns on words like 'lusty' (its meaning, 'vigorous', itself can have a sexual connotation) and 'active'.

The Yeoman

The military

The Yeoman is a forester by calling, and an archer in war. (Archery was proving crucial in defeating the mounted knights of the French.) Although he is quite anonymous (and is not given a tale to tell), note the clarity and detail of Chaucer's description. What is the effect of his colouring (green and brown) and his repeated key words: 'sharp' and 'bright'?

The Yeoman is the first of the characters whose 'professional' competence is described in detail. In this, he too is a yardstick for later pilgrims, since he employs his skills in a dedicated and proper ('yeomanlike') fashion (line 106): we will see others exploiting or misusing their professional competence.

Chaucer

The Yeoman's medallion is the first of several items of jewellery that show where a pilgrim's allegiance lies. **St Christopher** was the patron saint of foresters. This, together with the mass of typical forester's gear, builds up a neat joke at the expense of Chaucer the narrator, who tentatively 'guesses', right at the end, that the Yeoman must be a forester!

The Prioress (Lines 118–162)

There was also a Nun, a Prioress (head of a priory of nuns),
Whose smile was most simple/unaffected and coy/modest;
120 Her greatest oath was only 'By Saint Loy (Saint Eligius)';
And she was called [cleped] Madame Eglantine.
She sang the divine service/liturgy very well,
Intoned through the nose in a most seemly manner,
And she spoke French very well and elegantly [fetisly],
125 After the school of (ie with the accent taught at) Stratford-Bow,
For the French of Paris was unknown to her.
At table [mete] she was well taught/bred too [with alle];
She let no morsel fall from her lips,
Nor [ne] wet her fingers (by dipping them) deeply in her sauce;
130 Well could she carry a morsel (to her mouth) and take good care [wel kepe]
That not a drop fell upon her breast.
She took the greatest pleasure [lest] in courtesy/courtly manners.
She wiped her upper lip so clean (or so entirely)
That in her cup there was not (to be) seen one farthing/bit
135 Of grease, when she had drunk a draught.
She reached [raughte] for her food [meat] most decorously [semely].
And certainly [sikerly] she was very gay (or entertaining) [of greet desport]
And most pleasant, and amiable/friendly in bearing [port],
And (she) took pains to counterfeit/imitate the behaviour [cheere]
140 Of court, and to be stately/dignified in manner,
And to be held worthy [digne] of reverence/respect.
But, to speak of her sensibility [conscience],
She was so compassionate [charitable] and pitying/soft hearted
She would weep, if she saw a mouse
145 Caught in a trap, if it were dead or (if it) bled.
She had/kept (a number) of small dogs [hounds] that she fed
With roasted flesh/meat, or milk and fine white [wastel] bread.
But she wept sorely if one of them died,
Or if men/someone smote/struck it smartly/sharply with a stick [yerde];
150 And she was all sensitivity and tender heartedness.
Her wimple was gathered [pynched] most decorously (becomingly?) [semely],
Her nose well-formed, her eyes grey as glass;
Her mouth very small, and also [thereto] soft and red;
But certainly [sikerly] she had a fair/fine forehead;
155 It was almost a span broad, I think [trowe];
For, certainly [hardily], she was not undergrown/diminutive.
Her cloak was very elegant, as I noticed [was war].
She bore/carried on her arm a set [peire] of small coral
(Rosary) beads, with 'gauds' (every eleventh bead) of green,
160 And on it hung a shining golden brooch,
On which there was first written/inscribed a crowned 'A',
And after/below, '*Amor vincit omnia*' ('Love conquers all').

The Prioress

The clergy

Chaucer the pilgrim is charmed by the Prioress's courtly manners and personal beauty: he describes her, and quotes (presumably) her own account of her tender-heartedness, with an innocent fascination – and no sense of incongruity. Chaucer the poet observes her with a more satirical eye – but in the gentlest and most respectful manner.

Stratford-Bow probably refers to the Benedictine convent of St Leonard's in Middlesex. The comment on the Prioress's un-Parisian French may be a gentle swipe at her pretentions – or a joke at Chaucer the narrator's expense, hinting at his own intellectual snobbery.

'Simple' and 'coy' were typical traits of a heroine of courtly romance, as were the Prioress's looks (lines 151ff), and even her name (which means

Food and drink

'Sweetbriar'). **Saint Eligius** (her only oath) was famed for beauty and courtly behaviour, which is her own 'greatest pleasure'. The Prioress's table manners (lines 127ff) are almost a prescription for fashionable ladies of the time. (Note how Chaucer uses eating and drinking to reveal a character's preoccupations: a recurring theme.)

The Church

The Prioress thus follows the Knight and Squire as an 'ideal' of courtly romance – but with a difference, as the rhyming of 'coy'/'St Loy', and 'Eglantine'/'divine' should remind us. Although there is nothing immoral in her aspirations or behaviour, they are distinctly *un*spiritual. The recurring words 'port', 'cheere', and 'manere' make her preoccupations seem superficial. Note other ambiguous words which can (or should) have religious connotations – but do not. The Prioress's 'conscience' is not moral, but sentimental: even then, it seems to be directed entirely towards animals, not people. She is 'charitable' in the same sense.

Visual detail is used to suggest lapses in discipline. Feeding dogs on delicacies (line 147) is extravagant, and keeping dogs was specifically against the rule. The Prioress's 'fine forehead' should not have been visible: a **wimple** was supposed to cover the brow, cheeks and throat. The golden brooch hints at worldly vanity and a romantic sensibility – and sits oddly with rosary beads, which are used in prayer. But there is still no real suggestion of immorality: **'Amor'** is divine love, as well as human. It is a question of context: contrast the appropriateness of the Yeoman's dress and piece of jewellery with the faint incongruity of the Prioress's.

The Prioress's key word is 'semely' (lines 123, 136, 151), which means both 'fittingly/decorously' and 'becomingly/attractively'. This central ambiguity accounts for the gentleness of Chaucer's satire: the Prioress's behaviour is as attractive in the woman as it is unfitting in the nun.

The Prioress's companions (Lines 163–164)

With her she (the Prioress) had another Nun,
Who was her secretary-assistant [chapeleyne], and three Priests.

The Monk (Lines 165–207)

165 There was a Monk, an outstandingly [for the maistrye] fine fellow [fair],
     An outrider (inspector of monastery estates), who loved hunting [venerie],
     A manly man, fit [able] to be an Abbot (head of an abbey).
     He had many a dainty/fine horse in the stable,
     And when he rode, men/people could hear (the bells on) his bridle
170 Jingling in a whistling wind as clearly
     And also [eek] as loudly as the chapel bell.
     Where [ther as] this lord was keeper/head of the cell/sub-monastery –
     The Rule of Saint Maurus or of Saint Benedict
     Being old (fashioned) and somewhat [somdel] strict –
175 This same [ilke] Monk let old things/ways pass away/slide,
     And followed [heeld after] the new world/order of things, meanwhile [the space].
or And kept [heeld] the latitude/freedom [space] of [after] the modern world.
     He did not give a plucked [pulled] hen for that text
     That says that hunters are not holy men,
     Or that a monk, when he is heedless (of the Rule),
180 Is like a fish out of water –
     That is to say, a monk out of his cloister.
     But that same [thilke] text he held/considered not worth an oyster;
     And I said his opinion was good/sound.
     Why [what] should he study and make himself mad [wood],
185 Always poring over a book in the cloister,
     Or toil [swynken] with his hands, and labour,
     As Augustine bid/commanded? How shall the world be served?
     Let Augustine keep his toil [swynk] for himself!
     Therefore he (the Monk) was a real mounted hunter (or hard rider) [prikasour]:
190 He had/kept greyhounds as swift as birds [fowel] in flight;
     In tracking (or hard riding) [prikyng] and hunting the hare
     Was all his pleasure [lust], for he would spare no expense.
     I saw his sleeves (were) edged [purfiled] at the hand/cuff
     With 'grys' (a costly grey fur), the finest in the land;
195 And, to fasten his hood under his chin,
     He had a most elaborate [curious] pin/brooch wrought/made of gold;
     There was a love-knot at the larger end.
     His head was bald, and shone like glass,
     And likewise [eek] his face, as (if) he had been anointed (with oil).

The Prioress's companions

One Nun's Priest tells a tale later. If there were 3, however, this would bring the number of pilgrims to 31, when there are only supposed to be 29 (line 24). This is one of the small inconsistencies which Chaucer never revised.

The Monk

Chaucer begins with a typical assertion that this Monk is outstanding – and then mentions hunting. This sets the tone: the hunting monk was a familiar target of satire, and of more serious condemnation by the reformers. Like the Prioress, the Monk's sins are worldly rather than vicious, but they reflect declining standards in the Church. Look for hints of lapses from each of them of their vows of poverty, chastity and obedience!

The clergy

St Benedict was the founder of Western Monasticism, setting up his first community at Monte Cassino in AD 529. **St Maurus** was his discipline.

Note the range of Chaucer's satirical methods. The innocent narrator dwells on superficially impressive details of which the monk is clearly proud: his 'manliness' and jaunty kit (lines 167–71), his hard riding (189), and his costly clothes (193–96). The narrator recounts the Monk's forthright liberal views with approval (lines 177–88). All the time, however, the poet

undermines this simple-minded acceptance. We are asked to note logical inconsistencies (does 'manliness' really make an abbot?) and incongruities (the monk's fashionable bridle jingles like the chapel bell, the symbol of a neglected life of prayer). Once again, costly clothes and jewellery reveal inappropriate values. The Prioress also had 'gold': notice, as you read on, which (and how few) characters do *not*!

Vice

The satire is broadest as Chaucer describes the Monk's spirited defence of his freedom. The proverbial expressions for worthless objects (**'plucked hen'**, **'oyster'**) are jolly and colloquial, but in context, as the reported words

of a monk, what impression do they make? Consider the question in line 184: why *should* he study and toil? The narrator hardly seems to notice his own answer – that St Augustine made this the foundation of the monastic rule. (Another complaint of the reformers was that monks avoided work.) The question in line 187 ('What use would monks be to the world if they stayed in the monastery all the time?')

The Church

reveals both the Monk's worldliness and the approving narrator's stupidity: monks were not supposed to be of use to the world, but withdrawn from it.

Note Chaucer's richly ironic use of words. For example, the Monk's head shone 'as if he had been anointed' (line 199). Actually, he had: when he entered the ministry of the church. But you would hardly notice that!

The Monk (continued)

200 He was a lord/dignitary well-fattened and in good condition [point];
His eyes protruding [stepe], and rolling/restless in his head,
They gleamed [stemed] like a furnace/fire under a lead (cauldron);
His boots supple, his horse in perfect condition [estaat].
Now certainly he was a fair/fine prelate (senior cleric).
205 He was not pale as a tormented [forpyned] ghost.
Of all roast meats, he loved best a fat swan.
His palfrey/riding-horse was as brown as a berry.

The Friar (Lines 208–269)

There was a Friar, a wanton/sportive and merry fellow,
A limiter (licenced to beg in a district or 'limit'), a very festive [solempne] man.
210 In all the four Orders (of friars) there is none that knows [kan]
So much of dalliance/small-talk and flattery.
He had made/arranged many a marriage
For young women, at his own expense.
He was a noble pillar of his Order.
215 He was well-loved and familiar/on easy terms
With franklins (landowners) throughout his begging district [contree],
And also [eek] with women of standing [worthy] in the towns;
For he had the power/authority to take confession (and grant absolution),
As he said himself, more (of more serious sins) than a parish priest [curat],
220 For he was a licentiate of his order (licenced to do so by the Pope).
He heard confession most sweetly,
And his absolution was pleasant:
He was an easy man (when it came) to give penance,
Where he knew [wiste] he would get a good pittance/donation.
225 For to give [yive] to a poor (religious) order
Is a sign that a man is well shriven (has made a good confession);
For if a man gave (alms), the Friar dared assert [make avaunt],
He knew the man was truly repentant;
For many a man is so hard of heart,
230 He cannot weep (for his sin), although it grieves [smerte] him sorely.
Therefore instead of weeping and prayers
Men must give silver to the poor friars.
His tippet/cape was always stuffed [farsed] full of knives
And pins, to give to fair women [wyves].
235 And certainly he had a merry/pleasant singing voice [note];
He knew well how to sing and play on a rote (a stringed instrument);
At singing ballads [yeddynges] he took the prize outright.
His neck was white as the fleur-de-lys/lily;
Moreover he was as strong as a champion/fighting man.

The Monk (continued)

Food and drink

The Monk's appearance supports the attractive openness and verve of his hunting – along with its worldliness. He is clearly a gourmand: another example of food as an indicator of temperament. The comedy is broad and fairly affectionate: the man is 'well-fattened' – like his favourite dish! 'Roast' rhymes comically with 'ghost', and 'forpyned' here means 'wasting away with suffering'.

> Again, Chaucer makes an ambiguous word the key to the character: 'venerie' (line 166) means hunting, but with a faint echo of both 'venality' (corruption) and 'venerial' (of Venus, the goddess of love).

The Friar

The clergy

Chaucer's satire is less affectionate in the case of the Friar. He is clearly corrupt, and his lechery and avarice (making money out of the sacrament of penance) are serious, 'mortal' sins.

The **four Orders** (line 210) were the Dominicans, Franciscans (founded by St Francis), Carmelites and Augustinians, or Austin Friars.

Vice

One of the Friar's sins is sexual immorality. Chaucer begins ambiguously: 'wanton' can mean sportive/merry, but also undisciplined and, as today, promiscuous. Extravagant praise (line 210) is once again swiftly undermined: the Friar is superior, not in vocation, but in flirtation. Note how unsavoury he seems as a lover compared to the Squire (a comparison further invited by his white neck and ballad singing). Lines 212–13 suggest that he put up dowries to marry off women he had seduced. 'Noble pillar' sounds like a phallic pun. Later, he is said to be 'well-loved and familiar' with prosperous women (line 217) and to carry small gifts for his conquests (lines 233–34). A white neck (line 238) and a lisp (264) were the marks of licentiousness, according to contemporary theories.

The Church

The unprincipled Friar was a familiar target of satire and protest. Friars' notorious laxity in imposing penance (in return for donations) was a source of resentment for parish priests, who (lines 218–19) were not licensed to grant absolution in serious cases, as some friars were. The Friar is the first of the pilgrims who is explicitly ruled by avarice. Chaucer the narrator naively approves his conduct of the sacrament (no doubt echoing the Friar's own self-praise) as 'sweet', 'pleasant' and 'easy'. But Chaucer the poet, rhyming 'penance' and 'pittance', makes it clear that this amounts to bribery: the Friar let people off easily for a fee (or in the case of the women, a favour). The Friar's justification of his avarice (that giving money is the only sure way to tell that a man is truly repentant) is clearly a sign of hypocrisy.

The Friar (continued)

240 He knew the taverns well in every town
   And every innkeeper [hostiler] and barmaid [tappestere]
   Better than a lazar/leper or a beggar-woman;
   For to such an eminent [worthy] man as he
   It was not fitting [acorded not], in respect of his position [facultee],
245 To have acquaintance with sick/diseased lepers.
   It is not respectable [honest], it can be to no advantage,
   To have dealings with such poor folk [poraille],
   But only with rich (people) and sellers of victuals/provisions.
   And above all, wherever profit was to arise/be had,
250 He was courteous and humble [lowely] in offering his services.
   Nowhere was there any man so capable [vertuous].
   He was the best beggar in his house;
   [And gave a fixed rent [ferme] for the licence [graunt] to beg;
   None of his brethren entered his territory [haunt];]
   For though a widow had not a shoe,
   So pleasant was his '*In principio...*' ('In the beginning...'),
255 That he would still get a farthing/small coin, before he left.
   His gains [purchas] were a lot better than his rent (he paid the convent).
   And he could romp [rage], just like a puppy [whelp].
   On love/settlement days, he could be a great help (as arbiter of disputes),
   For there he was not like a resident of a cloister
260 With a threadbare cloak (or vestment), like a poor student,
   But like a Master (of Arts or Divinity) or a Pope.
   His half-cope/short cloak was of double worsted (wool),
   And rounded as a bell out of the mould [presse].
   He lisped a little, out of affectation [wantownesse],
265 To make his English sweet upon his tongue;
   And when he played the harp, when he had sung,
   His eyes twinkled in his head just [aryght]
   As do the stars in the frosty night.
   This fine [worthy] limiter/friar was called [cleped] Hubert.

The Friar (continued)

The Church

The bitterness of Chaucer's satire deepens as he describes the Friar's scorn of the poor and sick: the very people he is meant to serve (as the portraits of the idealised Parson and Ploughman later make clear). Chaucer is at his most sarcastic in lines 243ff. The narrator reports – without comment – the Friar's view that he is too 'worthy' (eminent or distinguished) to have dealings with the poor and diseased. This is not 'worthy' in the high moral sense in which the word was used of the Knight: it has been grotesquely distorted, like the Friar's sense of right and wrong. It is in fact precisely 'fitting' (line 244) that he should spend time with the poor. Instead, his motives are entirely mercenary. The contrast with the Knight is reinforced by the words 'courteous', 'humble' and 'service': the Friar is capable of such virtues only when profit is to be had. 'Vertuous' (line 251) is another one of Chaucer's words which should have moral and religious connotations – but, in context, does not: here it means simply capable, and refers to the Friar's prowess in begging.

Virtue

The irony is further reinforced by Biblical references in lines 253–5. The poor widow giving her small coin features in the gospel as an example of sacrificial generosity and faith (Mark 12:43): in this case, the small coin is conned out of the poor woman, by the Friar's charm and the power of his position. (**In principio** is the opening of John's Gospel: 'In the beginning was the Word…'. The verses were held to have a mystic power of their own.)

Line 256 has been variously interpreted. It could mean that the Friar's gains were more than the 'ferme' he paid for his licence to beg: ie, he made a profit. It was also a proverbial expression, that his 'gains' added up to more than his 'income': ie, he made illegal pickings on the side.

The bumbling narrator, impressed with the Friar's worldly substance, appears to see none of this, and instead takes a snobbish swipe at the 'poor student' in his 'threadbare cloak' (line 260): a little later, just such a student will be one of the poet's most respected (because least worldly) characters. Note that the Friar's cloak is bell-like: impressive, but hollow. His description ends with a clash between 'worthiness' and 'wantonness', 'sweetness' and 'frost'.

The Church

In profiting from popular preaching, friars were the rivals of pardoners: Chaucer's Friar and Pardoner both tell tales in the style of sermons. The Friar also manages to infuriate the Summoner with his tale about a summoner carried off by the devil after being cursed by one of his victims: the Summoner retaliates with the tale of a crooked limiter. The Friar, despite his position with the regular clergy, is thus linked with the corrupt church officials in the final group of pilgrims.

The Merchant (Lines 270–284)

270 There was a Merchant with a forked beard,
   In motley (multi-coloured cloth), and he sat (on a) high (saddle) on his horse.
   On his head a Flemish beaver (fur) hat,
   His boots clasped neatly and elegantly [faire and fetisly].
   He spoke his opinions [resons] most solemnly/impressively,
275 Proclaiming [sownynge] constantly the increase of his profit [winning].
   He wished [wolde] the sea to be guarded [kept] at all costs
   Between Middelburg (on the Dutch coast) and Orwell (on the Suffolk coast).
   He well knew how to sell écus [sheeldes] (French coins) on the exchange.
   This estimable [worthy] man put [bisette] his wits to very good use:
280 No person [wight] knew [wiste] that he was in debt,
   So stately/dignified was he in his conduct,
   In his dealings [bargayns] and his lendings and borrowings [chevyssaunce].
   Forsooth/truly he was a worthy man, too [with alle].
   But, truth to tell, I do not know [noot] what he was called.

The Clerk (Lines 285–308)

285 There was also a Clerk (ecclesiastical student) from Oxford.
   Who had long ago/since (moved on) to (the study of) logic.
   His horse was as lean/skinny as a rake,
   And he was not all that fat, I swear [undertake],
   But looked hollow (cheeked), and also serious [sobrely].
290 His topmost [overeste] short-coat [courtepy] was very threadbare;
   For he had not yet got himself a benefice/Church living,
   Nor was worldly enough to take secular employment [office].
   For he would rather [hym was levere] have at his bedhead
   Twenty/a score of books, bound in black (calf) or red (sheepskin),
295 Of Aristotle and his philosophy,
   Than fine robes, or fiddle, or gay psaltery/lyre.
   But although he was a philosopher (also 'alchemist'),
   He still had but little gold in his coffer/chest.
   But all that he could get [hente] from his friends,
300 He spent on books and on learning,
   And busily/diligently did [gan] pray for the souls
   Of those [hem] that gave him (the money) with which to study [scoleye].
   Of study he took most care [cure] and most heed.
   He spoke not one [o] word more than was necessary,
305 And that was said with (due) formality [forme] and respect,
   And short/brief and lively [quyk] and full of lofty meaning [hy sentence];
   His speech/discourse was in tune with [sownynge] moral virtue
   And he would glady learn and gladly teach.

The Merchant

The bourgeoisie

Why is the Merchant first among lay pilgrims, since the Sergeant-at-Law and Franklin would have outranked him? Perhaps because Chaucer wished to establish (as he did with the Knight) a standard for those to follow: in this case, the epitome of middle class, money-centred values.

The description briefly conveys the Merchant's essential qualities, while progressively deflating him. First we see the prosperous display; then the boasting and fretting about his money; then hints of shady dealing. Only royal moneychangers were allowed to profit from currency exchange. Perhaps the Merchant's 'lendings' included financing the Crown: 'bargayns' and 'chevyssaunce' often referred to dishonest deals. The word 'worthy' is again used ironically. As usual, Chaucer gives apparent praise (line 279) – only to disclose that the 'good use' of the Merchant's wits was disguising his debts. (The foolish narrator says 'no man knew' about this – but he has learned about it after an evening's gossip at 'The Tabard'!)

> In summing up, the narrator appears to be casting about for something to say. Do you think he is clumsily 'backing off' from identifying his Merchant, having hinted at illegal dealings? Or has he just found him rather dull?

The Clerk

The bourgeoisie

Virtue

Oxford was already an established university in the fourteenth century. (We learn that the Clerk had also been at Padua in Italy, another major seat of learning.) **Logic** was the main subject of philosophical study in an Arts course.

The Clerk provides a stark contrast, positioned between the Merchant and Sergeant-at-Law, to the worldly values of these two men – and the regular clergy who precede them. The Clerk and his horse are lean: unlike the Monk. His coat is threadbare: the Friar's was not. His heart is set on study, as it should be (line 303): unlike the three regulars, whose 'pleasure' was in inappropriate things. His speech is 'sownynge' in moral virtue (line 307): contrast the Merchant's 'sownynge' the increase of his profits.

'Twenty books' is meant as a round (and very large) number: twenty actual volumes would have cost the same amount as two or three houses!

Alchemists (lines 297–8) searched for the so-called 'philosopher's stone' which could turn base metals into gold. This is a gentle joke, not really at the Clerk's expense. He is one of the few characters (like the Knight) who is explicitly *not* associated with gold, and does not seek it. How do you think Chaucer regards the Clerk, from the tone of the portrait as a whole?

The Sergeant-at-Law (Lines 309–330)

A Sergeant-at-Law (legal officer), cautious [war] and wise/prudent,
310 Who had often been at the porch of St Paul's (where lawyers consulted) [parvys],
There was also, most rich in excellence.
He was discreet and of great distinction –
He seemed (to be) such/so, his words were so wise.
He had often acted as judge [justice] at the assizes [county courts],
315 By letters patent (from the King) and by general warrant [pleyn commissioun].
For his knowledge [science] and for his high renown/reputation,
Of fees and robes (from clients) he got many a one [oon].
Nowhere was there so great a purchaser/buyer (of land):
Everything was 'fee simple' (outright ownership) to him, in effect;
320 His title (to the land) could not be proved invalid [infect].
Nowhere was there so busy a man as he,
And yet he seemed busier than he was.
He knew precisely [in termes] all the legal cases and judgements
That had happened [falle] since the time of King William (the Conqueror).
325 Moreover, he knew how to compose [endite] and draw up a deed [thyng],
In which no one [no wight] could fault [pynche at] his writing;
And he knew every statute (Act of Parliament) completely [pleyn] by heart [rote].
He rode only plainly dressed [hoomly] in a medley/motley (mixed-weave) coat
Girt/belted with a girdle [ceint] of silk, with narrow bars/stripes;
330 I am saying no more about his attire [array].

The Franklin (Lines 331–360)

A Franklin (landowner) was his (the Sergeant-at-Law's) companion.
His beard was as white as the daisy;
In his temperament [complexioun] he was 'sanguine'.
In the morning [morwe] he really loved a sop/piece of bread (dipped) in wine;
335 To live in delight/pleasure was always his wont/custom,
For he was a true son of Epicurus (an 'epicure'),
Who held the opinion that pure [pleyn] delight/pleasure
Was true [verray] and perfect felicity/happiness.
He was a householder, and a great/major one;
340 In his district [contree] he was Saint Julian (patron saint of hospitality).
His bread, his ale, were always of one standard [after oon] (ie uniformly good);
Nowhere was there a man with a better wine-cellar [envyned].
His house was never without baked-meats/pasties
Of fish and meat [flessh], and so plentiful, (that)
345 In his house, it snowed food [mete] and drink,
And all the delicacies [deyntees] that men/one could think of.
According to the sundry/various seasons of the year,
He changed his food and his supper/dinner.

The Sergeant-at-Law

The Sergeant is the most eminent of the upper-middle class pilgrims: a man genuinely at the top of his profession. Described as 'rich in excellence', he is also making money from his clients. He buys land for himself: this suggests both that he has more substance than the Merchant (whose fortune is less securely invested) and that he aspires to join the landed gentry. Note how understated his dress is: a sign of very discreet wealth. Remember that the Knight was 'worthy' (brave) and 'wys': what is the effect of line 309?

Chaucer knowledgeably describes the professional prowess of the Sergeant: like the Yeoman, he is defined by his competence. He is expert in both branches of English law: case law (decisions given in the courts) and statute (legislation). He uses his skills to his own advantage — eg, in gaining unrestricted ownership of land — but there is no suggestion of corruption.

> Chaucer very subtly undermines the Sergeant. The key word is **'semed'**. Lines 313 and 322, following the narrator's usual praise in a deceptively casual way, are very telling. The Sergeant seemed a man of distinction: why only 'seemed'? A vivid twist to the old distrust of lawyers! We suspect that the impressive list of the Sergeant's knowledge was supplied by the man himself.

The Franklin

The Franklin is a complete contrast to his companion: where the Sergeant was discreet and careful, the Franklin is jolly and extravagant.

Complexion refers to body chemistry. It was believed at the time that matter was made up of four elemental qualities (hot, cold, moist and dry) which in the human body combined in four 'humours': blood (hot and moist); phlegm (cold and moist); yellow bile or choler (hot and dry) and black bile (cold and dry). Predominance of blood created a sanguine 'complexion': phlegm, phlegmatic; yellow bile, choleric and black bile, melancholic. One sign of a sanguine complexion was a ruddy face: the rhyme of 'sangwyn' with 'wyn' cheekily suggests where some of that redness may have come from!

Epicurus was an Athenian philosopher (341-270 BC) who considered pleasure to be the chief good of man. He actually stressed the need for self-control and overcoming outward circumstances, but his followers, the Epicureans, emphasised self-gratification and particularly the pleasures of the table — which the Franklin certainly appreciates. Food and drink dominate this portrait with cheerful exaggeration: the house positively 'snows' delicacies.

Food and drink

The Franklin (continued)

He had a great many fat partridges in the coop [muwe],
350 And many a bream and pike [luce] in the fishpond [stuwe].
Woe to his cook unless [but if] his sauce was
Piquant [pognaunt] and sharp, and all his utensils [geere] to hand.
His permanent [dormant] table in his hall always
Stood ready covered all day long.
355 At sessions (of the Justices of the Peace) he was lord and master [sire] (ie presided);
Very often, he was 'knight of the shire' (Member of Parliament for the county).
A short dagger [anlaas] and a purse [gipser] all of silk
Hung at his girdle/belt, white as morning milk.
He had been a sheriff (the King's administrator in the shire) and an auditor.
360 Nowhere was there such a distinguished [worthy] landowner [vavasour].

The Guildsmen (Lines 361–378)

A Haberdasher and a Carpenter,
A Weaver [webbe], a Dyer, and a Tapicer/tapestry-maker –
And they were clothed all in one and the same [o] livery
Of a solemn and great/important fraternity/guild.
365 Their gear/equipment was fresh and newly adorned [apiked];
Their knives were mounted [chaped] not with brass
But entirely with silver; wrought/made most neatly [clene] and well
(were) their girdles and their pouches/purses altogether[everydeel].
Each of them seemed a suitable [fair] burgess/citizen
370 To sit on the dais/platform in a guildhall (with the mayor and aldermen).
Each one [everich], for the wisdom that he knows/has,
Was fit [shaply] to be an alderman.
For they had enough property [catel] and income [rente],
And also [eek] their wives would heartily assent/agree to it;
375 Else/otherwise, certainly they (the wives) were deserving of blame.
It is most pleasant [fair] to be called [ycleped] 'madame',
And go to vigils (services on the eve of festivals) in front of everyone [al bifore],
And have a mantle/cloak royally borne/carried (for you).

The Cook (Lines 379–387)

They (the Guildsmen) had with them for the occasion [nones] a Cook
380 To boil the chickens with the marrowbones,
And tart/sharp flavouring powder [poudre-marchant] and sweet cyperus [galingale].
He well knew how to [koude] recognise [knowe] a draught of London ale.
He knew how to roast, and seeth/boil, and broil/grill and fry,
Make mortreux (thick soups), and bake a good pie.
385 But it was a great pity [harm], it seemed [thoughte] to me,
That he had on his shin a sore (a dry-scabbed ulcer) [mormal].
For he made white-meat pudding [blankmanger] with the best of them.

The Franklin (continued)

The Franklin does not need to be motivated by money, like the other bourgeois pilgrims. The reference to Saint Julian (line 340) established that

Vice

he is not gluttonous, but generous in his hospitality: he has a table permanently set for company. Self-gratification is a decidedly more attractive weakness than avarice: Chaucer's indulgence is suggested by the innocence of the Franklin's 'daisy-white' beard and 'milk-white' purse, and the pride and relish with which he has (we assume) described his provisions to the narrator. How do you imagine the Franklin? Chaucer leaves room for a jolly, childlike figure before adding (line 355) that he has in fact been a judge, MP and sheriff: a distinguished public career. How do you read the word 'worthy' in the Franklin's case?

The Guildsmen

The bourgeoisie

The Guildsmen are almost entirely anonymous here, and are not given tales later. Since the men represent different crafts, but all wear the same livery (or uniform), they must belong to a social or religious guild. A **haberdasher** was a maker of small articles of dress, such as buttons and ribbons.

The main satire is reserved for the common (and soft) target of the Guildsmen's wives. Once again, the innocent narrator misses the point, when he says that they would be wrong not to agree to their husbands' appointments as aldermen (line 375): it was far more likely to be the ambitious wives pushing their husbands into it! Note how Chaucer parodies the wives' social aspirations: 'royally' is deliberately over the top. The whole portrait is one of carefully-paraded wealth and social climbing. Do you find it rather predictable, after the other descriptions?

The Cook

The bourgeoisie

Food and drink

The Cook's name is Roger. Although his tale is unfinished, he is given a star turn towards the end of the pilgrimage when, stupified with drink, he falls off his horse. Chaucer shows a typically confident familiarity with culinary matters, but the Cook's repertoire seems a little basic, compared with the Franklin's kitchens. (On the pilgrimage, the Host teases him about his shoddy pies and unhygienic cook-shop.) In this brief description, Chaucer adds two subversive elements. First, that the Cook could 'recognise' a draught of London ale: he certainly does during the pilgrimage! Rather worse, there is the uncomfortable closeness of the ghastly 'mormal' and the white-meat (chicken) pudding...

The Shipman (Lines 388–410)

There was a Shipman/Sea-Captain, living [wonynge] far to the west;
For aught/as far as I know [woot], he was from Dartmouth.
390 He rode on a carthorse (or nag) [rouncy], as (well as) he was able,
In a gown of falding (a coarse woollen cloth) to the knee.
He had a dagger hanging/slung on a cord [laas]
Around his neck, down under his arm.
The hot summer had made his hue/colouring quite brown;
395 And certainly he was a good fellow/comrade (or 'lad').
Many a draught of wine had he drawn/carried/stolen
On the way from Bordeaux, while the merchant [chapman] slept.
He took no heed [keep] of nice/delicate tender feelings [conscience].
If he fought, and had/got the upper [hyer] hand,
400 He sent them (prisoners) home to every land – by water (ie he drowned them).
But concerning his skill [craft] at reckoning/calculating his tides,
His streams/currents, and the dangers/hazards around him,
His harbours and his moon, his pilotage (navigation) [lodemenage],
There was none such/like him from Hull to Cartagena (in Spain).
405 He was hardy/bold and wise/shrewd in (what he) undertook;
His beard had been shaken in many a tempest/storm.
He knew all the havens/harbours there were,
From Gotland (an island off Sweden) to Cape Finisterre (Spain),
And every creek/inlet in Brittany and in Spain.
410 His ship [barge] was called [ycleped] the *Magdalen*.

The Doctor Of Physic (Lines 411–444)

There was with us a Doctor of Physic/Medicine (a physician);
In all the world there was none like him,
In regard to medicine (or healing) [physic] and surgery,
For he had a grounding in astrology [astronomye].
415 He watched [kepte] his patient most attentively,
For the hours (most favourable for treatment), according to his 'natural' magic.
He was well able to calculate the most propitious moment [fortunen the ascendent]
(For making) images/talismans for his patient.
He knew the cause of every malady/illness,
420 Whether from hot, cold, moist or dry (elements),
And where (the illnesses) originated [engendred], and from what humour.
He was a true [verray], perfect/complete practitioner [praktisour]:
Once he knew the cause, and the root of his (the patient's) suffering [harm],
He immediately [anon] gave the sick man his remedy [boote].
425 He had his apothecaries/druggists very ready
To send him his drugs and remedies (medicaments) [letuaries],
For each of them made the other make a profit [wynne] –
Their friendship was not a recent thing [newe to bigynne].
He was well-versed in the old (authorities on medicine) Aesculapius
430 And Dioscorides, and also Rufus (of Ephesus),
Old Hippocrates [Ypocras], Hali (ibn el Abbas) and Galen,
Serapion, Rhazes, Avicenna,

38

The Shipman

The bourgeoisie

A ship called the *Maudelayne* was recorded in Dartmouth (already a major port) at this time, under a master named Peter Risshenden. The Shipman is a fairly typical figure: tanned, piratical and clearly no landsman – he is not at home on a horse (line 390). The expression **'good felawe'** is ambiguous: it could mean 'good companion' or, by extension, 'crony' and 'rascal'. In line 396, we can still not be sure that any rascality is implied, since 'ydrawe' can simply mean hauled or carried (the Shipman's trade): however, it can also mean drawn in the sense of taking a draught – or indeed stealing one! (The modern slang equivalent might be 'lifted'.) Line 397 makes it clear that the Shipman was defrauding the merchant whose

Vice

wine he was importing. Chaucer's father was in the wine trade, so perhaps this is a family joke – or even a past experience.

Chaucer makes a rather grimmer joke out of the practice of drowning prisoners. After that, however, the description is, like the Yeoman's, a straight exposition of admirable professional skill. **'Moon'** refers to its phases, which affect the tides, and **'lodemenage'** to the lodestar (North Star) by which sailors navigate. Note that, as a man of action, the Shipman echoes the Knight in his combined boldness and prudence (line 405).

The Doctor of Physic

The bourgeoisie

The Physician is the epitome of his profession: in describing him, the narrator resorts to hyperbole (line 412). Chaucer displays his knowledge of medieval medical science. **Astrology** was an accepted branch of medicine: planetary positions were held to influence the patient and the effectiveness of treatments. This **'natural' magic** was considered a science – not necromancy or 'black' magic. The **images** (line 418) may have been talismans of the signs of the zodiac, or a figure of the patient. **'Fortunen the ascendent'** meant to divine when the ascendant (the rising zodiacal sign) was in a favourable position, by the conjunction of the planets. The qualities which made up the **humours** (see 'complexion' on page 35) also combined to form the four **elements**: earth (cold and dry); air (hot and moist); water (cold and moist) and fire (hot and dry). Imbalances in the elements and humours were thought to cause illness: too much fire caused a fever, for example.

The innocent narrator praises the Physician as a 'true' and 'complete'

Vice

practitioner (echoes of the Knight) in line 422, because he is so swift to provide medicine. But having the druggists ready (line 425) is not just forethought. This is a jibe at a well-known racket: druggists put business the way of doctors who purchased medicines from them – so both parties benefited from the transaction.

The Doctor of Physic (continued)

Averroes, (Johannes) Damascenus and Constantinus (Afer),
Bernard (Gordon), and (John of) Gaddesden and Gilbertus (Anglicus).
435 He was moderate [mesurable] in his diet/what he ate,
For it was not superfluous/excessive,
But extremely nourishing/nutritious and digestible.
He did not study the Bible very much.
He was clad entirely in blood-red [sangwyn] and Persian blue [pers] cloth,
440 Lined with taffeta and fine silk [sendal];
And yet he was only slow [esy] in spending money [dispence];
He kept/saved what he won/made during the plague [pestilence].
For gold in medicine [phisik] is a great cordial/restorative,
So he loved gold especially.

The Wife Of Bath (Lines 445–476)

445 There was a good/worthy Wife/woman from near [biside] Bath,
But she was somewhat deaf, and that was a pity [scathe].
She had such a skill [haunt] in cloth-making,
She surpassed those of Ypres and Ghent (centres of the Flemish wool trade).
In all the parish, there was no woman [wif]
450 Who ought to precede her to (make) the offering:
And if (someone) did, she was certainly so angry [wrooth],
That she was (put) out of all charity (generosity *and* general goodwill).
Her kerchiefs/head-dresses were of a very fine texture [ground];
I dare swear they weighed ten pounds,
455 (The ones) that were on her head on Sundays.
Her hose/stockings were of fine scarlet red,
Tied/fastened very tightly [streite], and shoes quite supple [moiste] and new.
Her face was bold and fair/handsome and ruddy [reed of hewe].
She was a respectable [worthy] woman all her life:
460 She had had five husbands at the church door (where marriages were legalised),
Without/not counting other companionship in youth –
But it is not necessary [nedeth nat] to speak of that at present [as nowthe].
And she had been thrice to Jerusalem;
She had crossed [passed] many a foreign river [straunge strem];
465 She had visited Rome, and (the image of the Virgin) at Boulogne
(The shrine of) St James (of Compostella) in Galicia and (of the Magi) at Cologne.
She knew a lot [muchel] about wandering the way/travelling around.
To tell the truth [soothly], she was gap-toothed.
She sat easily/at ease on an ambling horse,
470 (Her brow, cheeks and neck) well covered by a wimple, and on her head a hat
As broad as a buckler or a shield [targe];
An outer skirt [foot-mantel] about her large/ample hips,
And on her feet a pair of sharp spurs.
In company [felaweshipe] she knew well how to laugh and talk [carp].
475 Doubtless [per chaunce] she knew about cures (or potions) [remedies] of love,
For of that art, she 'knew the oldest dances'/knew all the tricks.

The Doctor of Physic (continued)

Lines 429–34 give a panoramic view of medical authorities. **Aesculapius**, a Greek god, was patron of medicine, but **Hippocrates** was its founder: doctors still take the Hippocratic Oath of ethics today. The other names are Greek and Arabic writers, plus three 14th century Britons. After this, the portrait is more pointed. The Physician's diet is moderate and healthy, but

Food and drink

notice the rhyme 'digestible'/'Bible': he nourishes the body, but starves the soul. Despite his rich clothes, he does not (unlike the Franklin) share his wealth: a fact connected with his cynical profit from the plague. Note the heavily ironic explanation of his love of gold: it *was* actually used in medicines – but was a 'tonic' to the Physician in a different sense…

The Wife of Bath

The bourgeoisie

The Wife is one of Chaucer's best-loved and most memorable characters. The comedy is based on the stereotypical vain, lusty and domineering woman, but Chaucer also celebrates her abundant humanity and life. What is the effect of the word 'worthy' in this portrait, do you think?

The Wife's deafness was caused by a blow from her fifth husband (a 'toy boy', whom she spotted at her fourth husband's funeral!): he was so repentant that he let her rule the household. (Her tale is part of a debate on who should have authority in marriage: you can guess *her* view…)

The Wife is vain and self-important: fighting over precedence in church was a stock example of pride, here given an added twist by the ironic pun on lack of 'charity'. But she is joyously larger than life. Her clothes are flamboyant, endearingly outdated and clearly intended to advertise her wares (not just as a clothmaker)! Required to cover her head in church, she goes

Vice

completely over the top (line 454). She is a boldly attractive woman, and the narrator is torn between his fascination with her colourful past (lines 460–61) and belated discretion (line 462). Having recounted the Wife's many pilgrimages, he notes – almost straight-faced – that she has 'been around' (line 467). He then adds, apologetically, that she is 'gap-toothed':

a sign of luck and travel – but also (as the Wife says in her own bawdy Prologue) the mark of Venus, goddess of love. In lines 475–76, the narrator gives way to an open, indulgent wink at her experience. What is the effect of 'shield' and 'spurs' in this context? (Such warlike details, along with physical curiosities like the gap teeth, are a feature of Chaucer's description of the 'lower' pilgrims.)

The Wife later confesses that she goes on pilgrimages for pleasure, to see and be seen: not an uncommon reason, since pilgrimages were the nearest thing to escorted tours. What motives have the other pilgrims had?

Pilgrimage

The Parson (Lines 477–528)

There was a good religious man,
Who was a poor village [toun] Parson/priest,
But he was rich in holy thought and deed [werk].
480 He was also a learned man, a clerk/scholar,
Who would truly preach Christ's gospel;
He would devoutly teach his parishioners.
He was benign/kindly, and wonderfully diligent/hardworking,
And most patient in adversity,
485 Which was proved/put to the test many times [ofte sithes].
He was loath/reluctant to excommunicate [cursen] for the sake of his tithes,
But, without a doubt, he would rather give [yeven]
To the poor parishioners around him
(Out) of the offering and also his (own) property [substaunce].
490 He knew how to have sufficiency/be content with little.
His parish was wide/extensive, and the houses far apart [asonder],
But he never omitted [lefte], in rain or thunder,
Sickness or mishap [meschief], to visit
The furthest (people) in his parish, great [muche] and small [lite],
495 On foot, and in his hand a staff.
This noble example he gave to his sheep,
That first he practised [wroghte], and then he preached.
He took [caughte] those words out of the gospel (of Matthew),
And this figure/image he added to it as well,
500 That if gold rusts, what will iron do?
For if a priest, in whom we trust, be foul/tainted,
No wonder an ignorant [lewed] man 'rusts';
And it is a shameful thing – let priests take heed [keep] –
(To see) a befouled [shiten] shepherd and a clean sheep.
505 A priest really should give/set an example,
By his cleanness/purity, how his sheep should live.
He (the poor parson) did not put his benefice/living up for hire
And leave his sheep encumbered/struggling in the mire/mud (of sin)
While he ran to London to Saint Paul's
510 To find himself a chantery (endowment to sing a daily mass) for (departed) souls,
Or to be retained [witholde] by a brotherhood/guild (as chaplain);
But (he) dwelt at home, and guarded [kepte] well his (sheep) fold,
So that the wolf did not make it come to harm [myscarie];
He was a shepherd, and not a mercenary/hireling.
515 And although he was holy and virtuous,
He was not scornful [despitous] towards sinful men/folk,
Nor arrogant [daungerous] nor haughty [digne] in his speech/discourse,
But courteous [discreet] and benign/kindly in his teaching.
To draw/lead folk to heaven by holy living [fairnesse],
520 By good example – this was his endeavour [bisynesse].

The Parson

The clergy

The Parson joins the Knight as another ideal figure: conspicuously, the only member of the clergy to do so. He too is described in terms of virtue and action, rather than dress or food – reflecting his own spiritual focus. He is placed among the sinful laity he serves, rather than among his worldly colleagues: he has renounced the position and wealth they cultivate. Chaucer praises virtues, and condemns abuses, emphasised by the reformer Wycliffe. The Sergeant-at-Law later calls the Parson a Lollard, and he does show a Wycliffean emphasis on Scripture and personal responsibility before God (lines 527–8), but he also embodies more general Christian ideals.

Virtue

Note the Parson's virtues: faith (line 477), diligence (483), patience and fortitude (484–5), charity (487), temperance (490), justice (497), purity (506), humility and courtesy (line 515–8), tolerance (516, 526). How did the Prioress, Monk and Friar measure up in each of these specific areas? What about the Knight? The Parson's key quality is that he leads by example, practising what he preaches (lines 496, 505, 520 and 528): a pointed contrast to the hypocrisy that is rife amongst almost all the other pilgrims. Chaucer points out that the gospel (Matthew 5:19) puts practice before preaching: the first of a series of Biblical references which remind us that Christ is the focus of this Parson's life.

The Church

Note the abuses of the clergy's position which – unlike many of his contemporaries – the Parson avoids: threatening excommunication for non-payment of tithes (line 486); laziness in ministry (line 492); renting out his living to a vicar or curate or – worse – leaving the parish unattended, while he ran off to find a 'cushy' and well-paid post in London (lines 507–11).

Virtue

Two traditional metaphors are central to the Parson's portrait. The ideal of the Christian minister was the **Good Shepherd**, an image used by and of Jesus himself. The gospel (John 10:11-13) says that he is faithful in looking after his sheep, and when the wolf (the devil) attacks, he fights to the death to protect them, unlike a hired hand, who runs away: compare lines 509 and 512–14. There is a pun on 'mercenary' (hired hand) too: a 'chappelain mercenaire' was a priest who made a living purely from saying Mass.

The other image is based on the proverb: 'if **gold** (supposedly pure) rusts, what will iron (a baser metal) do?' Chaucer clearly explains this, to show that a priest has an obligation to set a good example. He also links both metaphors in the idea of purity or cleanness: rusted gold is like a befouled (literally, with dung – 'shiten') shepherd. Note the complex use of the word 'foul', meaning both dirty (including rust) and wicked: in other words, tainted – physically and morally.

The Parson (continued)

Except for an obstinate person (persisting in sin):
Whatever (type of person) he was, of high or low estate/rank,
He (the Parson) would rebuke [synbben] him sharply on the spot [for the nonys].
A better priest, I believe [trowe], does not exist anywhere.
525 He expected [waited after] no pomp/ceremony or reverence/deference,
Nor were his sensibilities [conscience] over-refined [spiced] (or fastidious),
But the lore/doctrine of Christ and his twelve apostles
He taught – but first he followed it himself.

The Ploughman (Lines 529–541)

With him (the Parson) there was a Ploughman (who) was his brother,
530 Who had hauled [ylad] many a load [fother] of dung/manure;
He was a good and faithful [trewe] labourer [swynkere],
Living in peace and perfect charity/love for his fellow men.
He loved God best/first with all his heart
At all times, whether it pleased [gamed] or pained [smerte] him (ie in good times or bad),
535 And then/next (he loved) his neighbour as himself.
He would thresh, and also make ditches [dyke] and dig [delve],
For the sake of Christ, for any poor person [wight],
Without payment [hire], if it lay within his power.
He paid his tithes fairly/honestly and in full [wel],
540 Both on (the fruits of) his own labour [propre swynk] and on (the increase of) his property [catel].
He rode in a tabard (labourer's smock) on a mare.

There was also a Reeve and a Miller,
A Summoner and a Pardoner too,
A Manciple and myself – there were no others [namo].

The Miller (Lines 545–566)

545 The Miller was a stout/strong fellow [carl] indeed [for the nones];
He had huge muscles [brawn] and bones too.
That was certainly proven, for wherever [over al] he went [cam],
He would always win [have] the ram (the prize) in the wrestling.
He was short-shouldered/stocky, broad, a thickset, sturdy type [knarre];
550 There was no door he was unwilling to [nolde] heave off its hinges [of harre],
Or break (down) by running at it (or 'at one charge') with his head.
His beard was red as any sow or fox,
And broad, too, like a spade.
On the very [right] tip [cop] of his nose he had
555 A wart, and on it stood/grew a tuft of hairs,
Red as the bristles of a sow's ears;
His nostrils were black and wide.
He bore/carried by his side a sword and buckler.
His mouth was as great/wide as a great/gaping furnace (door).

The Parson (continued)

Although he is tolerant towards his parishioners, the Parson is not complaisant: he rebukes sinners when required. At the end of the Tales, it is he who recalls everyone's thoughts to the true nature of pilgrimage. As with the Knight, the narrator's superlatives (line 524) here ring true.

The Ploughman

The bourgeoise

Virtue

The Ploughman may be the Parson's real brother, or simply a fellow Christian. Either way, he complements the ideal Christian minister with the ideal Christian layman: an example of how spiritual values can be applied in everyday life. The ploughman hero of Langland's poem *Piers Plowman* is much like this (and is also linked to the Good Samaritan and Christ). Chaucer's Ploughman's portrait is full of Biblical resonances which, ironically, expose the clergy's failings. 'Good and faithful labourer' echoes Jesus's parable of the talents (Matthew 25) where the master commends his 'good and faithful' servants: at the same time it recalls the Monk's contempt for labour. 'Charity' is the highest of all Christian virtues (1 Corinthians 13): it also reminds us of the Prioress's charity – to mice! The layman serves the poor: contrast with this the Friar's attitude. The Ploughman loves God first, with all his heart, then his neighbour as himself: the two greatest commandments, according to Jesus (Matthew 22).

Tithes were payable on wages earned for labour and on other gains, such as increases in flocks and herds. The Ploughman is not prosperous: a mare was a humble mount, and he rides in labourer's clothes. What gives him the dignity with which he comes across in his portrait?

> The introduction of the final pilgrims as a group suggests a connection between them. Popular tradition would readily identify it as rascality: the joke is that Chaucer includes himself among these social dregs.

The Miller

The bourgeoise

The shock of contrast, after the Parson and Ploughman, is extreme. The Miller is a grotesque figure: brutish, powerful, menacing. He is described in an intensely physical way: consider the expressive effect of words like 'brawn' and 'bones', and 'thikke knarre' (pronouncing all the 'k's). Note the animal associations and the slightly hellish red and black colouring. The Miller's physical characteristics are unattractively vivid. According to contemporary theories of physiognomy (the practice of judging character from facial features), they were also (like the Wife of Bath's teeth) significant. A stocky figure, a red, bushy beard, and a flat nose with a wart on top were associated with shamelessness, loquacity, aggression and lechery: spot on for the Miller!

The Miller (continued)

560 He was a chatterer [janglere] and a coarse buffoon (or jester) [goliardeys],
And that (his talk) was mostly scurrilous and bawdy.
He well knew how to steal corn and charge [tollen] three times (the proper amount);
And yet, by God [pardee] he had a golden thumb (he was honest, for a miller!).
He wore a white coat and a blue hood.
565 He knew well how to blow on and sound/play a bagpipe,
And with that he led us out of town.

The Manciple (Lines 567–586)

There was a worthy [gentil] Manciple of an inn of court [temple],
From whom purchasers (in catering) [achatours] might take (their) example
(Of how) to be wise/shrewd in the buying of victuals/provisions;
570 For whether he paid (cash) or took (the goods) on credit [by taille],
In every way [algate] he kept such an eye on [wayted] his buying [achaat]
That he was always ahead (of the game) [biforn] and in a good position [staat].
Now is that not a most clear [fair] (example of the) grace of God
That such an unlearned [lewed] man's wit shall outdo [pace]
575 The wisdom of a heap of learned men?
He had more than thirty [thries ten] masters (of Law) (to provide for),
Who were expert and skilled [curious] in the law,
Amongst whom there were a dozen in that house
Worthy/capable of being stewards of (managing) the revenue [rente] and land
580 Of any lord/peer in England,
(In such a way as) to make him live on his own [propre] income [good]
Honourably free of debt [dettelees] – unless he were mad [wood] -
Or live as frugally [scarsly] as he pleased;
Capable [able] too to help an entire shire/county
585 In any (emergency) situation [caas] that might occur [falle or happe];
And yet this Manciple made fools [sette hir cappe] of them all.

The Reeve (Lines 587–622)

The Reeve was a slender, choleric man.
His beard was shaved as close [ny] as he could (get it);
His hair was shorn/close-cropped all round his ears [erys];
590 His top (hair) was docked/cut short in front [biforn] like a priest's.
His legs were very long and very lean/thin,
Like [ylyk] a staff/stick, no calf was visible [ysene].
He could take good care of [kepe] a granary [gerner] and a (corn) bin;
There was no auditor who could get the better of him [him wynne].
595 He knew [wiste] well by the drought and rain(fall)
The (likely) yield [yeldynge] of his seed and grain.
His lord's sheep, his cattle [neet], his dairy (cows),
His swine/pigs, his horses, his livestock [stoor] and his poultry
Were wholly/entirely in this Reeve's control [governynge],
600 And according to his contract [covenant] he gave an account [rekenynge] (of it all),
(Ever) since his lord/master was twenty years of age.

The Miller (continued)

Millers notoriously abused their monopoly on grinding corn. The proverb ran: 'An honest miller has a golden thumb'. Following the Knight's tale, the Miller – already drunk – rudely breaks in with a coarse, funny story about the cuckolding of a carpenter (making fun of the Reeve, who trained as one). How does *The General Prologue* prepare us for this development?

Vice

Chaucer himself includes a brief flash-forward to the journey of the following day: we learn that the Miller leads the group as they set out.

The Manciple

A manciple was an obscure character, and this one is entirely anonymous. Most of his portrait is taken up with description of his masters. But this is the key to its success: Chaucer paces it carefully for effect.

The bourgeois

It begins with a typical passage of praise for the Manciple's professional excellence. Like the Sergeant-at-Law, another purchaser, the Manciple is 'wys', or shrewd, but there is no reason to suspect his honesty. We learn that his wit outdoes his masters' wisdom, but this could simply be more approval from our impressionable narrator, who attributes the Manciple's success to the grace of God. (Ironically, in the light of his later disclosure that the Manciple cheats his masters!) Throughout the catalogue of the lawyers' capabilities (lines 577–85), it seems possible that Chaucer is building up to the conclusion that the Manciple is even more capable than them. But finally, we reach the punchline: he has been making fools of them all. (We assume he buys cheaply and keeps the rest of the money for himself.)

The Reeve

The Reeve (whose name is Oswald) at first seems similar to the Manciple, but his abuse of his master's trust is more extreme. Once again, Chaucer does not immediately disclose malpractice, but praises the way the Reeve keeps the grain stores and estimates the yield from the crops. The fact that no auditor (inspector of the accounts) could get the better of him may simply mean that he kept the books in good order.

The bourgeois

But there is something 'mean' about the Reeve's looks. (In the prologue to his tale, he says he is old and has a 'mouldy heart'.) Cropped hair was a sign of his servile position, but it reinforces the austere impression created by his skinniness. These features were, according to the physiognomists, typical of a **choleric** complexion (predominance of the hot and dry humour, yellow bile). They denoted sharpness of wit (which we see later), and irascibility and lechery (to which he confesses in his own prologue).

The Reeve (continued)

No one could lead him into (or prove he was in) arrears [arrerage].
There was no [nas] bailiff, nor herdsman, nor other servant,
Whose trick [sleighte] and dodgy deal [covyn] he did not know;
605 They were afraid [adrad] of him as of death (itself).
His dwelling [wonyng] was most handsome, (set) on a heath;
His place (also manor-house) was shadowed/shaded by green trees
He knew better than his lord/master how to purchase/buy (land).
He had amassed a rich store (of goods), secretly [pryvely];
610 He was expert at subtly/cunningly pleasing his lord,
By giving and lending him (some) of his (the lord's) own property [good],
And getting thanks, and a coat and hood (as reward) besides [yet].
In (his) youth he had learned a good trade [myster];
He was an excellent workman [wrighte], a carpenter.
615 This Reeve sat upon an excellent stallion [stot]
Which was all dapple [pomely] grey, and called [highte] Scot.
He had on a long surcote/outer coat of Persian blue (cloth),
And by his side he bore/carried a rusty blade.
This Reeve, of whom I tell, was from Norfolk,
620 Near a village men call [clepen] Bawdeswell.
He (wore his coat) tucked/hitched up around him [aboute] like a friar [frere],
And he always rode the hindmost/last of our band [route].

The Summoner (Lines 623–668)

There was a Summoner with us in that place,
Who had the fiery-red face of a cherubim,
625 For he was pimply [saucefleem], with narrow eyes.
He was as hot and lecherous as a sparrow,
With scaled/scabby black brows and sparse [piled] beard.
Children were frightened [aferd] of his face.
There was no quicksilver/mercury, litharge (protoxide of lead) nor brimstone,
630 Borax, ceruse (white lead), nor any oil/cream of tartar,
Nor ointment that would cleanse and bite/burn,
That could help (cure) him of his white blotches [whelkes],
Nor of the lumps (pimples) [knobbes] sitting on his cheeks.
He adored garlic, onions and also leeks,
635 And to drink strong wine, red as blood;
Then he would speak and cry/shout as (if) he were mad [wood].
And when he had drunk a lot of wine,
(Then) he would speak not a word except Latin.
He had/knew a few terms/tags, two or three,
640 That he had learned from some (legal) decree –
No wonder, he heard it all day;
And besides [eek] you know well how a jay
Can (be taught to) cry [clepen] 'Wat' (Walter) as well as the Pope.

The Reeve (continued)

With the ambiguity of line 602, the tone changes. There is unpleasant irony

Vice

in the fact that the Reeve knows the 'sleighte and covyn' (also 'cunning and deceit') of his underlings: we are about to learn about his own. Whether or not he uses his knowledge against them (which may be implied), they fear him like death itself: a chilling note. The Reeve's hypocrisy is emphasised by the contrast between his tyranny and the pleasant graciousness of his house. This also suggests that he is somehow feathering his own nest, a suspicion confirmed in line 609. Sole control over the property and accounts allows the Reeve to skim off money and goods, on top of the legitimate rewards of his position, like a house. The Reeve even lends back to his master money that he has stolen from him, and is thanked and rewarded for it! Do you sense an ironic note of admiration for the sheer audacity of the scheme? What is the effect of the comment that the Reeve had a good trade and was an 'excellent workman' in his youth?

> There was traditional enmity between millers and reeves. Our Miller tells his tale of a cuckolded carpenter on purpose to annoy the Reeve. The latter retaliates with a tale of a crooked miller (very like the pilgrim) who is swindled himself. The Reeve's rusty dagger may imply that he is not a man of action – which may also account for the fact that he rides at the opposite end of the band from the brawny and hot-tempered Miller!

The Summoner

The clergy

As a church officer, the Summoner arguably belongs higher up the social scale, but in the moral order – and popular esteem – he deserves his place here. Chaucer abandons ambiguity and the amiable irony of the narrator's perspective: the Summoner's portrait is loaded with distaste and sarcasm.

Food and drink

His offputting appearance makes an immediate impact. The reference to **'cherubim'** is ironic: they were commonly depicted with red faces – but there is nothing otherwise 'angelic' about the Summoner! His skin eruptions, scabby brows and thinning hair were all symptoms of the disease alopecia, a form of leprosy: the treatments Chaucer mentions were those used at the time. His condition would have been worsened by strong food and wine. What impression is created by his favourite foods?

Vice

The Summoner is first described as a lecher (line 626) and a drunkard (lines 635ff). And he is not a jolly drunk: he shouts crazily and spouts pretentious nonsense in the few words of Latin he has picked up in the courts. (A jay was taught to cry 'Wat' in the way that a parrot is taught to say 'Polly'.) He is both vicious and stupid: a profoundly unattractive combination.

The Summoner (continued)

But if anyone was able to test [grope] him further [in oother thyng],
645 Then he had spent/exhausted all his philosophie;
He always cried: '*Questio quid iuris*' ('The question is, what part of the law applies').
He was a charming [gentil] rascal [harlot] and a kind one:
A better fellow (*or* more complete rogue) one could not find.
For a quart of wine he would allow [suffre]
650 Any rogue [good felawe] to keep a concubine/mistress
For a twelvemonth/year, and pardon [excuse] him completely [atte fulle];
He himself knew how to pluck a finch ('pull a bird'!) on the quiet [prively].
And if he found anywhere a like-minded rogue [good fellawe],
He would teach him to have no awe/fear
655 In such a case (living in sin) of the archdeacon's curse (of excommunication),
Unless a man's soul were in his purse;
For it was in his purse that he would be punished (by a fine or bribe).
'Purse is the archdeacon's hell,' said he.
But I know [woot] well that in fact he lied completely;
660 Each guilty man ought to dread being excommunicated [cursynge] –
For excommunication slays (the soul) just as absolution [assoillyng] saves (it) –
And also beware of a *Significavit* (imprisonment as a result of excommunication).
He had in (his) control [daunger], subject to his own whim [gise],
The young people [girles] of the diocese,
665 And knew their counsel/secrets, and was their only adviser [reed].
A garland had he set upon his head
As big as (if) it were for (the top of) a tavern signpost [ale-stake].
He had made himself a buckler/shield out of a loaf [cake] (of bread).

The Pardoner (Lines 669–714)

With him (the Summoner) there rode a noble [gentil] Pardoner
670 From (the hospital of St Mary) Rouncivalle, his friend and comrade [compeer],
Who had come straight from the (papal) court at Rome.
Loudly he sang 'Come hither, love, to me!'
The Summoner accompanied him with a strong [stif] bass ('ground') melody [burdoun];
There was never a trumpet [trompe] of half so great/loud a sound.
675 This Pardoner had hair as yellow as wax,
But it hung as straight as a bunch (or skein) [strike] of flax (or its thread);
Such locks/hair as he had hung in little bunches [ounces],
And he spread it out (to cover) his shoulders;
But it lay thinly, in separate (single) [oon and oon] shreds [colpons].
680 But for fun [jolitee] he wore no hood,
For it was trussed/packed up in his wallet.
He thought he rode (out) all in the newest/latest fashion [jet];
Dishevelled/loose-haired, he rode bare-headed save/except for his cap.
He had staring (or shining) [glarynge] eyes like a hare.
685 He had a vernicle (copy of St Veronica's handkerchief) sewn on to his cap.

The Summoner (continued)

The words 'gentil' (used in the sense of 'noble', for the Knight) and 'kind' (a key quality of the Parson) highlight Chaucer's sarcasm: the Summoner is the epitome of the rogue (line 648) so this is a supreme anti-compliment. The Summoner is 'kind' because he lets offenders off the hook, for a modest bribe. He is corrupt not only in the performance of his duties, but in his personal conduct: 'plucking a finch' refers to his own sexual immorality. He is part of a corrupt system: lines 657ff reflect the notorious crookedness of the

The Church

ecclesiastical courts, using the threat of excommunication and its consequences to extort money. (**'Significavit'** was the opening word of the writ by which excommunicated people were handed over to the civil authorities.) In the Summoner's cynicism, Chaucer drifts perilously close to heresy – which he hastens to disown in line 659.

> The expressive effect of lines 656–58 can only be appreciated by reading them aloud. The word 'purse' echoes obsessively, from the rhyme position at the end of the first line, to the middle of the next, to the strong first syllable of the third, with the explosive effect of a contemptuous outburst.

Lines 663–65 may imply that the Summoner corrupts the young people, or that he uses their secrets to blackmail them – or both. The viciousness robs the drunken silliness which follows of any joy or attraction.

The Pardoner

The clergy

The phrase 'noble pardoner' is straight sarcasm on Chaucer's part: pardoners were notoriously corrupt – even the properly licenced ones who carried genuine papal indulgences. Many more were simply frauds: **Rouncivalle** pardoners were a particular target for satire, after the unauthorised sales of pardons by men professing to be collecting for the hospital. Chaucer's Pardoner obviously claims to have come straight from Rome, and the narrator takes this at face value. However, from what we learn later, it seems likely that he is a charlatan, and his pardons false.

> Note that 'Rome' and 'to me' rhyme. A two-syllable rhyme was considered clever. What effect is created by the rhyming of these particular words?

The Pardoner is as physically distinctive – and unsavoury – as his friend the Summoner. His hair, hanging in thin, dead-straight hanks, is faintly unhealthy-sounding, and mocks his vanity: note that he 'thought' he looked fashionable with it loose. A **vernicle** (a copy of a handkerchief pressed to Christ's face, and said to bear its image) was the badge of a pilgrimage to Rome: 'proof' that the Pardoner had come from there, as he claimed?

The Pardoner (continued)

His wallet lay in front of him in his lap,
Brimful [bretful] of pardons/indulgences, come hot(foot) from Rome.
He had a voice as thin (and high) [smal] as a goat has.
He had no beard, and never would have;
690 (His chin) was as smooth as if it were lately shaven.
I believe he was a gelding (castrated male horse) or a mare (female horse).
But at his craft/trade, from Berwick (in the north) to Ware (in the south),
There was not another Pardoner like him.
For in his wallet [male] he had a pillowcase [pilwe-beer],
695 Which he said was Our Lady's veil:
He said he had a piece [gobet] of the sail
That Saint Peter had, when he went (walked)
On the sea, until Jesus Christ caught hold of [hente] him.
He had a cross of latten (mixed metal) (studded) full of (fake gem) stones,
700 And in a glass he had pigs' bones (supposedly the bones of saints).
But with these 'relics', when he found
A poor parson dwelling/living in a country parish [upon lond],
In one day he got himself more money
Than the parson got in two [tweye] months;
705 And thus, with feigned flattery and tricks [japes],
He made the parson and the people his apes/dupes.
But to tell (you) truly at the last,
In church he was a noble ecclesiast/cleric.
He knew well how to read a lesson (portion of Scripture) or reading [storie],
710 But best of all [alderbest] he sang an Offertorium (after the Creed in Mass);
For well he knew [wiste], when the song/anthem had been sung,
He must preach and smooth [afilen] his tongue
To win silver (from the congregation), as he well knew how;
Therefore he sang more merrily [murerly] and loudly.

Recapitulation (Lines 715–724)

715 Now I have told you truly [soothly] and briefly [in a clause]
The rank [estaat], the attire [array], the number and also the cause/reason
Why this company/group was assembled
In Southwark at this excellent [gentil] hostelry
That was called [highte] the Tabard, close [faste] by the Bell (another inn).
720 But now it is time to tell you
How we conducted ourselves (ie what we did) that same night,
When we alighted/settled in that hostelry;
And afterward, I will tell of our journey [viage]
And all the rest [remnaunt] of our pilgrimage.

The Pardoner (continued)

Another mention of Rome: do you hear the echo of a sales pitch in line 687?

The description of the Pardoner's voice and smooth chin suggests that he is a eunuch, as the narrator (with uncharacteristic lack of charity) confirms in line 691. His sexual neutrality contrasts him strongly with characters like the Squire and the Wife of Bath, who are more immediately attractive.

The Church

Note the heavy sarcasm in the assertion that 'there was not another Pardoner like him': the characteristic formula is no longer complimentary. This Pardoner is the very best at what he does: conning innocent priests into buying false relics for their churches! The catalogue of the supposed relics makes it quite clear that they are shabby, far-fetched fakes: we are to assume that the Pardoner has openly joked about his victims' gullibility and his own cleverness, and boasted of the money he has made.

Vice

In the extraordinarily frank prologue to his tale, the Pardoner admits that his relics are false and his motives entirely mercenary. His tale is then a highly effective sermon *exemplum* proving that '*Radix malorum est cupiditas*' (avarice is the root of evil)! He freely admits to preaching, hypocritically, against his own pet vice, ironically noting that as a 'vicious man', he can still tell a 'moral tale'. Afterwards, he cynically tries to sell his (admittedly fake) pardons and relics to his fellow pilgrims! The enraged Host has to be calmed down by the Knight.

Line 708 may be taken as sarcasm – or grudging recognition of the Pardoner's preaching ability. Cynical and mercenary though his motives are (lines 712-13), he shows a genuine talent.

> The Pardoner's corruption is more sinister than the Summoner's, because it is coldly deliberate, without the excuse of drunkenness or stupidity. The Pardoner is highly self-aware, admitting in his prologue to avarice, malice, hypocrisy and gluttony – with an unrepentant pride that was considered the real root of all mortal sin.

Recapitulation

The narrator announced back in lines 35–42 that he was going to describe

Pilgrimage

each of the pilgrims before proceeding with events. Here, he sums up what he has just told us, and reminds us of the situation as we left it, with the pilgrims gathered at 'The Tabard' in Southwark. This is very much in the oral tradition of story-telling. The audience needs some orientation, in order to listen effectively. It also needs a breather from time to time!

Apology (Lines 725–746)

725 But first I pray/beg you, of/by your courtesy,
    That you do not attribute [arette] it to my bad manners [vileynye],
    If I speak plainly in this matter,
    To tell you their words and their behaviour [cheere],
    Nor if I speak their words exactly [proprely].
730 For you know every bit as well as I,
    (That) whosoever shall tell a tale/story after another man,
    He must repeat [rehearce] as closely [ny] as ever he can
    Every word, if it is his responsibility [charge] (to do so),
    Though the man speak never so rudely and broadly/freely,
735 Or else he must tell his tale untruly/falsely,
    Or feign/invent things, or find new words.
    He cannot spare/relent, even if (the man) were his brother;
    He must say one word as accurately [wel] as another.
    Christ himself spoke very broadly/freely in Holy Writ/Scripture,
740 And you know [woot] well that there is no coarseness [vileynye] (in His words).
    Moreover, Plato says, (for) whoever is able to read him,
    That the words must be cousin to the deed.
    Also I pray you to forgive me,
    That I have not set/placed folk in their rank [degree]
745 Here in this tale, as they should stand.
    My wit is short (I am not very bright), you may well understand.

The Host (Lines 747–768)

    Our Host (the innkeeper) gave every one of us a most friendly greeting [chiere],
    And sat us down to supper/dinner immediately [anon].
    He served us with the finest victuals/food;
750 The wine was strong, and it pleased [leste] us well to drink.
    Our Host was withal/moreover a man fit [semely]
    To have been a marshal (master of ceremonies) in any hall.
    He was a large/big man with prominent [stepe] eyes –
    There is no finer (or handsomer) [fairer] burgess in Cheapside –
755 Bold/racy in his speech, and wise/shrewd, and well-schooled [ytaught] (in manners),
    And in regard to manhood/manliness, he lacked absolutely nothing.
    And moreover he was indeed a merry/cheerful man,
    And after supper he began to play/jest,
    And spoke of mirth/amusement amongst other things,
760 When we had paid our bills [maad our rekenynges],
    And said thus: 'Now, masters [lordynges], truly,
    You are most heartily welcome to me/my house;
    For by my troth/on my honour, I tell no lie,
    I have not seen this year so merry a company/group
765 In this lodging (inn) [herberwe] at one time [atones] as (there) is now.
    Fain/gladly would I amuse you [doon yow myrthe], if I knew [wiste] how.
    And I have just now thought of an amusement [myrthe],
    To give you pleasure [doon yow ese], and it shall cost (you) nothing.

Apology

Chaucer

After the scathing satire of the Summoner's and Pardoner's portraits, Chaucer re-establishes himself in the character of the innocent narrator, by apologising (in advance) for anything offensive in his story. His excuse is fairly standard: Boccaccio offers a similar justification in the author's conclusion to The *Decameron*. Note the irony, however. Chaucer's excuse is that as narrator, he has a duty to report all his fellow pilgrims' words truly, exactly and fairly: if there is anything crude or offensive – well, that is how the pilgrims really spoke. The joke is, of course, that they didn't! Chaucer the poet is not reporting reality, but writing fiction: in fact, 'inventing things and finding new words' (line 736).

The precept from **Plato**, the great Athenian philosopher (*c.* 427-347 BC), comes from one of the 'dialogues' with his master, Socrates. Since St Augustine, Platonic (or neo-Platonic) ideas had been incorporated into Christian thought, so there is nothing odd about their pairing with Scripture. In any case, this is rather a learned reference for someone so allegedly simple-minded!

Chaucer also apologises for not placing his pilgrims in proper social order: he attributes the lapse to his lack of 'wit'. This is more than a simple joke at his own expense, since his ordering of the pilgrims is quite deliberate – and exhibits the sharpest wit of all. As we have seen, the positioning of the pilgrims relative to each other, and within the procession as a whole, often makes a clear point about their moral character and worthiness.

The Host

The Host

The Host (Harry Bailly) is himself a well-rounded character. Chaucer the pilgrim is typically impressed by his manly qualities and social skills. **Cheapside** was the marketplace of the City of London, and a more *up*-market place than Southwark: Chaucer is complimenting the Host by favourably comparing him with the citizenry there (line 754).

The key word for the Host is 'mirth' (jollity and amusement).

Food and drink

Note how often it, and related words like 'merry', crop up as the Host brings the pilgrims under his sway. He has often been seen as the embodiment of 'Merry England', the medieval social ideal of carefree feasting and fun. Later in the Tales, he seems a less ideal (though no less colourful) character. Already, another key word for him is 'wys' or shrewd. Do you think he has really 'just now thought' of the tale-telling contest (line 767) or is this a regular performance for pilgrim trade? Note that the game *will* cost the pilgrims something: (line 768): a meal at the Host's own inn!

The Tale-Telling Game (Lines 769–821)

You are going to Canterbury – Godspeed (may God give you success),
770 (And may) the blessed [blisful] martyr reward you [quite yow youre meede]!
And well I know [woot], as you go along the (pilgrim's) way/road,
You intend [shapen yow] to tell tales [talen] and to play/jest;
For truly, (it) is no comfort/pleasure nor mirth/amusement
To ride along the way/road as dumb/silent as a stone;
775 And therefore I will devise [maken] you an entertainment [disport],
As I said before [erst], and give you some pleasure [confort].
And if it pleases [liketh] you all, with one accord [assent],
To stand/abide by my judgement/decisions,
And to do [werken] as I shall tell you,
780 Tomorrow, when you ride along the way/road,
Now, by the soul of my dead/late father [fader],
If you are not merry, I will give you my head!
Hold up your hands (to show agreement), without more discussion [speche].'
It did not take long to seek/find out our opinion [conseil].
785 It seemed to us it was not worth making it (a matter of) wisdom (deliberating about it),
And (we) granted him (our consent) without more/further consideration [avys],
And bade him say/give his verdict [voirdit] as he pleased [hym leste].
'Masters,' quoth/said he, 'now listen [herkneth], to your advantage [for the beste];
But do not take/treat it disdainfully [in desdeyn], I pray you.
790 The point/object is, to speak briefly and plainly/clearly,
That each of you, to shorten our journey [weye] with,
Shall tell two [tweye] tales during this expedition [viage] -
On the way to Canterbury, I mean –
And on the way home he shall tell another two,
795 Of adventures that happened [bifalle] in the past [whilom].
And which(ever) of you acquits [bereth] himself best of (you) all -
That is to say, (he) who tells in this case/on this occasion
Tales with the best content [sentence] and most entertainment value [solaas] -
Shall have a supper/dinner at the expense [cost] of us all
800 Here in this place, sitting by this post/pillar,
When we return [come agayn] from Canterbury.
And in order to make you the merrier,
I myself will gladly [goodly] ride with you,
Entirely at my own expense [cost], and be your guide;
805 And anyone who would [wole] dispute [withseye] my judgement
Shall pay everything that we spend along the way/road.
And if you vouchsafe/agree that it be so,
Tell me immediately [anon], without more words/discussion,
And I will prepare myself [shape me] for it early/without delay.'
810 The matter [thing] was granted/agreed, and our oaths sworn
With most glad heart, and (we) prayed/begged him also
That he would vouchsafe/condescend to do (as he had said),
And that he would be our governor/leader,
And (be) judge of our tales and referee [reportour],

The Tale-Telling Game

The Host proposes a tale-telling contest to amuse the pilgrims on the road, and offers to go with them as guide and adjudicator. The pilgrims agree.

This is the first extended passage of direct speech we have heard. Notice the natural speech qualities (the oral style) of the poetry: additions and asides (line 769); the address to the listeners to gather their attention (788); rhetorical devices which have little expressive function, but allow the speaker and listeners breathing space (790); oaths (781); repetitions and explanations (796–97) and so on. Remember that Chaucer was writing within an oral (spoken) tradition: the appropriate stylistic effects can seem odd to a silent reader, but they come into their own again when we are invited to imagine *listening* to them spoken by one of the characters. The beauty of the tale-telling contest is that it allows Chaucer to exploit this effect all the time: the tales are being orally narrated to the audience of fellow pilgrims, and we the readers are merely invited to 'listen in'. As a hint of this, the word 'whilom' (line 795) is the equivalent of 'once upon a time': the Knight and Miller both use it to open their tales.

Pilgrimage

Note that Chaucer's original conception included four tales by each of the pilgrims. In the end, he did not get all the way through even a single round of stories. (See our notes on *Structure and sources*.) In any case, the Host has managed to turn a casual diversion of pilgrimage travel (lines 771–72) into a complete party game, which threatens to take over the pilgrimage altogether. There is little contemplative or penitential spirit in the journey envisaged by the Host. Do you think any of the pilgrims might have wanted to object to this hijacking of the pilgrimage's spiritual purpose (restored by the Parson at the very end of the tales)?

The Host

The Host overcomes any misgivings with his forceful personality and persuasive skill. He sounds so generous in wanting to entertain and guide the pilgrims that it is easy to miss the fact that he does not put up the prize for the tale-telling contest: the prize supper will be paid for by the losing pilgrims (lines 799–800), to the Host's benefit.

The wise and forceful guide was a familiar figure in contemporary literature, especially in the genre of dream-visions. Perhaps the most famous example is Dante's *Divine Comedy*, where the narrator is guided by the poet Virgil through hell and purgatory to heaven. Chaucer adds a comic touch by creating a mischievous, unpredictable, all-too-human guide, whom we later learn to be fond of wine and bawdy jokes, full of blood-curdling oaths and henpecked by his wife.

The Tale-Telling Game (continued)

815 And arrange a supper/dinner at a set [certeyn] price,
And we would be ruled by his will [devys]
In high and low (ie in all things); and thus by one accord [assent]
We agreed to abide by [acorded to] his judgement.
And with that, the wine was fetched immediately [anon];
820 We drank, and each one (of us) went to rest/bed,
Without tarrying/lingering any longer.

The Departure (Lines 822–858)

The next morning [amorwe], when day began to dawn [sprynge],
Up rose our Host, and was/acted as cock ('wake-up call') for all of us,
And gathered us together all in a flock,
825 And we rode forth at a little more than (walking) pace
To the watering (place) of Saint Thomas (on the Kent road);
And there our Host pulled up [bigan... areste] his horse
And said, 'Masters, listen [herkneth], if you please [leste].
You know [woot] your promise [foreward], and I recall [recorde] it to you.
830 If even(ing)-song and morning-song (matins) agree (you haven't 'changed your tune'),
Let us see now who shall tell the first tale.
As may [mote] I (as surely as I hope to) always drink wine or ale,
Whosoever rebels against my judgement/ruling
Shall pay for everything that is spent along the way/road.
835 Now draw lots (straws) [cut], before we go any further [ferrer twynne];
He who has the shortest shall begin/go first.
'Sir Knight,' quoth/said he, 'my master and my lord,
Now draw a straw [cut], for that is my agreement [accord].
Come nearer [neer],' quoth/said he, 'my lady Prioress.
840 And you, sir Clerk, forsake [lat be] your shyness [shamefastness],
And don't muse (sit in a brown study) [studien]; put (your) hand to (it), everyone!'
Immediately [anon] every person [wight] began to draw (their straws),
And to cut the story short,
Whether [were it] by luck, or fate, or chance
845 The truth is this, the lot [cut] fell to the Knight,
About which everyone [wight] was very happy and glad,
And he had to [moste] tell his tale, as was right [resoun],
By promise [foreward] and by agreement [composicioun],
As you have heard: what need (is there) for more words?
850 And when this/that good man saw that it was so (how things were),
As a man who [he that] was wise/sensible and obedient
To keep a promise [foreward] (given) with his free assent/consent,
He said 'Since I shall/must begin the game,
Why, (let) the draw [cut] be welcome, in [a] God's name!
855 Now let us ride (on), and listen [herkneth] to what I say.'
And with that word, we rode forth on our way,
And with a right merry/cheerful manner [cheere] he began
His tale straightaway, and said as you may hear (as follows).

The Tale-Telling game (continued)

The idea of a rash promise to abide by the rules of a game would also have been familiar: the Arthurian legend of *Sir Gawain and the Green Knight*, retold in a well-known contemporary poem, features just such a promise, regretted later when the game gets out of control. Do you sense something a little dangerous about the Host's leadership?

The Host

The Departure

The brief description of the pilgrims' waking up and setting off is full of the excitement of early-morning departures.

At the first stop to water the horses, we see again Chaucer's skill at reflecting a natural oral delivery: consider lines 828, 832 and 837, for example. We also see the Host's social skills in action, as he flatters the most eminent pilgrims, coaxes the shy Clerk out of his shell and generally chivvies everyone along.

Pilgrimage

There is no particular distinction to be made between **luck, fate and chance**, in line 844. The redundant repetition is fairly standard for a loose narrative style. However, it also emphasises the irony of the fact that luck had little to do with the Knight's drawing the short straw: it was deliberate – certainly on the part of Chaucer, and probably on the part of the socially-adept Host – to have the Knight tell the first tale. (It is worth noting, however, that ideas of fate and chance were central to contemporary debate – later discussed in the *Nun's Priest's Tale* – about whether God's fore*knowledge* of events meant that they were also pre*destined*, whether Man had free will, and how chance could operate within God's providence.)

> The final word in the General Prologue is left with the Knight, who demonstrates his fine qualities of good sense, faithfulness to his word, and cheerful and gracious manners. The tale-telling has begun!

Self-test Questions

Who? What? Why? When? Where? How?
1 Who is the 'hooly blisful martir' of Canterbury and why was he venerated?
2 Who are Zephyr; Epicurus; St Benedict; King William; and 'Olde Ypocras'?
3 What are the four humours and their corresponding 'complexions'?
4 What was the 'philospher's stone'?
5 Why does Chaucer apologise for what he has written and is about to write?
6 Why should people have feared the 'archdeacon's curse'?
7 Where do the pilgrims meet and what similar place is nearby?
8 Where were lawyers consulted; marriages legalised; 'indulgences' issued?
9 How did the Shipman 'send home' his prisoners?
10 How many Tales are each of the pilgrims apparently going to tell?

Who is this?
From your knowledge of the poem, identify the following pilgrims:
1 Who 'was as fresh as is the month of May'?
2 Who could 'rage... as it were right a whelp'?
3 Who 'of her smylyng was ful symple and coy'?
4 Who says: 'My wit is short, ye may wel understonde'?
5 Who was 'a manly man, to been an abbot able'?
6 Who 'was right a myrie man'?
7 Of whom is it said that 'though that he were worthy, he was wys'?
8 Who 'semed bisier than he was'?
9 Who 'koude muchel of wandrynge by the way'?
10 Who was 'riche... of hooly thoght and werk'?
11 Who seems like 'a geldyng or a mare'?
12 Who was 'a trewe swynkere and a good'?
13 Who 'at wrestlynge wolde have alwey the ram'?
14 Who says 'Purs is the erchdekenes helle'?
15 Whose speech is 'sownynge in moral vertu'?

Food for thought
Chaucer uses the motif of food and drink to reveal his pilgrims' preoccupations.
What does it reveal in the following cases?

1	The Prioress	2	The Monk
3	The Franklin	4	The Physician
5	The Summoner		

Clothes maketh the man
Clothes are also a telling indicator of character. What jewellery, adornment or accessory does each of the following pilgrims have, and why are they significant?

1	The Yeoman	2	The Prioress
3	The Monk	4	The Wife of Bath
5	The Pardoner	6	The Summoner

Verray parfit pilgrims?
1 Which six pilgrims embody the positive ideals of their types?
2 Which six pilgrims are described in terms of professional competence?
3 Which nine pilgrims exploit their position or professional skills dishonestly?
4 Which four pilgrims have reputations as lovers; as fighters; as musicians?

A rose by any other name
Give two alternative meanings for each of the following words, and indicate to which pilgrim(s) each might refer:

1	Worthy	2	Wys
3	Solempne	4	Good Felawe
5	Charity	6	Conscience
7	Semely		

What's the meaning of this?

Translate the following lines:

1   'He loved chivalrie, Trouthe and honour, fredom and curteisie.'
2   'And peyned hire to countrefete cheere of court.'
3   'This worthy man ful wel his wit bisette: Ther wiste no wight that he was in dette.'
4   'But greet harm was it, as it thoughte me, that on his shyne a mormal hadde he.'
5   'He was a janglere and a goliardeys.'
6   'Of cursyng oghte ech gilty man him drede, for curs wol slee right as assoillyng savith.'
7   'And yet this Manciple sette hir aller cappe.'
8   'He kepte his pacient a ful greet deel in houres by his magyk natureel.'
9   'Us thoughte it was noght worth to mayke it wys, and graunted hym withouten moore avys.'
10 'And whiche they weren, and of what degree, and eek in what array that they were inne.'

Church times

Chaucer highlighted issues in the Church of his day. Let's explore...

1   In what ways is the Prioress's conduct 'lax' and unspiritual?
2   What did Augustine's rule require monks to do? Pick four examples that show Chaucer's Monk's rather different attitude to life.
3   What four vices (each!) are suggested in the Friar, Summoner and Pardoner?
4   What four contemporary abuses does Chaucer's Parson *not* exploit?
5   In what three practical respects is the Ploughman an ideal Christian layman?
6   Suggest three pairs of rhymes which incongruously link spiritual and worldly matters, as an indicator of a pilgrim's wordliness.

Who's who?

Match each pilgrim to his/her characteristics, from the scrambled options.

Pilgrim	Key word	Clothes	Pleasure	Appearance
Knight	Hospitable	Beaver hat	Power	Lank, yellow hair
Prioress	Seeming	Smock	Food	Gap teeth
Clerk	'Seemly'	Bagpipes	Gold	Hollow cheeks
Lawyer	Fake	Hitched-up	Bawdy talk	Skinny calves
Physician	Brutish	Scarlet stockings	Men	Wart on nose
Merchant	Charitable	Threadbare	Manners	None
Ploughman	Miserly	Stained tunic	God	Daisy-white beard
Miller	Unworldly	Milk-white purse	Profit	Forked beard
Reeve	'Solempne'	Simple but costly	Learning	Small, red mouth
Franklin	'Worthy'	Dishevelled	Chivalry	None
Wife of Bath	Lusty	Silk and taffeta	Land	None
Pardoner	Subtle	Fluted wimple	Trickery	None

Self-test Answers

Who? What? Why? When? Where? How?

1   St Thomas Becket (17). Martyred 1170, associated with healing (18)
2   God of West Wind (5); Greek philosopher who said pleasure was the chief good (336); St Benedict, founder of a famous monastic rule (173); William the Conqueror (324); Hippocrates, founder of medical science (431)
3   Blood/sanguine; black bile/melancholy; yellow bile/choleric; phlegm/ phlegmatic (333)
4   Substance sought by alchemists to turn base metals into gold (297)
5   He has not put the pilgrims in proper rank order (744). He will 'have' to relate their words, however offensive (727)
6   Excommunication meant hell and imprisonment (661–62, 657)
7   'The Tabard Inn', Southwark, South London. 'The Bell Inn' (718-19)
8   Porch of St Paul's (310); church porches (460); papal court, Rome (687)
9   'By water' (ie by walking the plank...) (400)
10 Four each (794)

Who is this?

1	Squire (92)	2	Friar (257)
3	Prioress (119)	4	Chaucer (746)
5	Monk (167)	6	Host (756)
7	Knight (68)	8	Sergeant-at-Law (322)
9	Wife of Bath (467)	10	Parson (479)
11	Pardoner (691)	12	Ploughman (531)
13	Miller (548)	14	Summoner (658)
15	Clerk (307)		

Food for thought

1   Preoccupation with dainty manners (132)
2   Liking for comforts and rich food, not monastic austerity (200, 206)
3   Innocent love of pleasure and hospitality (335, 345)
4   Careful nourishment of the body, but not the soul (437–38)
5   Unhealthy excesses (634–36)

Clothes maketh the man

1   St Christopher medal and other 'badges' of forestry (115)
2   Rosary, inappropriately combined with worldly vanity and romance (160)
3   Gold pin with true-love knot: worldly values and 'manly' vanity (196)
4   Huge hat: comic, abundant vanity. Sharp spurs: mastery in love (471-73)
5   Vernicle: suggesting that he has just come from Rome (685)
6   Garland and 'buckler' of bread: drunken foolishness (668)

Verray parfit pilgrims? (Name any four)

1   Knight (chivalry); Squire (courtly lover); Yeoman (professional); Clerk (scholar); Parson (minister); Ploughman (Christian layman)
2   Yeoman; Sergeant-at-Law; Cook; Shipman; Physician; Reeve
3   Friar: exploits confessional (223,218). Merchant: illegal exchange (278,282). Shipman: stealing wine (397). Physician: scam with apothecaries (427). Miller: stealing corn, overcharging for grinding (562). Manciple: cheating on buying (586). Reeve: defrauding master, blackmailing servants? (609). Summoner: taking bribes; corrupting young (649,663). Pardoner: selling false pardons and relics (694)
4   Lovers: Squire, Friar, Wife of Bath, Summoner
    Fighters: Knight, Squire, Yeoman, Shipman, Miller
    Musicians: Squire, Friar, Miller, Summoner and Pardoner

A rose by any other name

1 Valiant (Knight); respectable (Wife); eminent, pompous (Merchant)
2 Prudent (Knight, Shipman); cautious or shrewd (Sergeant-at-Law, Manciple)
3 Festive (Friar); imposing – or pompous (Merchant); solemn (Guildsmen)
4 Good companion – or rogue (Shipman, Summoner)
5 Love of fellows (Ploughman); generosity (Wife of Bath – ironically); tender-heartedness (Prioress)
6 Moral sense (Parson); tender-heartedness (Prioress) neither (Shipman)
7 Fitting/decorous or becoming/attractive (Prioress)

What's the meaning of this?

1 He loved chivalry, loyalty and honour, generosity and courtesy (46)
2 And took pains to imitate courtly behaviour (139)
3 This worthy man put his wits to very good use: no one knew that he was in debt (279)
4 But it was a great pity, it seemed to me, that he had a sore on his shin (385)
5 He was a chatterer and a coarse buffoon (560)
6 Guilty men should fear excommunication, for it kills just as absolution saves (660)
7 And yet this Manciple made fools of them all (586)
8 He watched his patient most attentively for the most favourable times for treatment, according to his natural magic (415–6)
9 It did not seem to us worth deliberating, and we agreed without more discussion (785)
10 And what type they were, and of what rank, and also what attire they wore (40)

Church times

1 She keeps dogs; does not cover her brow; is extravagant and vain; concentrates on courtly manners; her 'charity' is sentimental, and not aimed at people
2 Study and work (184–85) Four from: bridle bells (169); 'venerie' (166); contempt for the rule (177); hard riding (189); roast swan (206)
3 Friar: sexual licence (212), avarice (224), contempt for the poor (246), worldliness (259). Summoner: lechery (626), drunkenness (635), corruption (649), heresy (654), hypocrisy (651). Pardoner: vanity (682), fraud (694), avarice (703), hypocrisy (714)
4 Excommunicating for tithes (486); laziness (492); absenteeism (507); laxness (523)
5 Faithful work (531); work for the poor (537); tithing honestly (539)
6 Three from: pulled hen/hooly men (177); cloystre/oystre (181); penaunce/pittance (223); sho/in principio (253); digestible/Bible (437); purs/curs (655)

Who's who?

Pilgrim	Key word	Clothes	Pleasure	Appearance
Knight	'Worthy'	Stained tunic	Chivalry	None
Prioress	'Seemly'	Fluted wimple	Manners	Small, red mouth
Clerk	Unwordly	Threadbare	Learning	Hollow cheeks
Lawyer	Seeming	Simple but costly	Land	None
Physician	Miserly	Silk and taffeta	Gold	None
Merchant	'Solempne'	Beaver hat	Profit	Forked beard
Ploughman	Charitable	Smock	God	None
Miller	Brutish	Bagpipes	Bawdy talk	Wart on nose
Reeve	Subtle	Hitched-up	Power	Skinny calves
Franklin	Hospitable	Milk-white purse	Food	Daisy-white beard
Wife of Bath	Lusty	Scarlet stockings	Men	Gap teeth
Pardoner	Fake	Dishevelled	Trickery	Lank, yellow hair

■ Writing an examination essay

Take the following to heart

● *Carefully study each of the questions set on a particular text* Make sure you understand what they are asking for so that you select the one you know most about.

● *Answer the question* Obvious, isn't it? But bitter experience shows that many students fail because they do not actually answer the question that has been set.

● *Answer all the question* Again, obvious, but so many students spend all their time answering just part of a question and ignoring the rest. This prevents you gaining marks for the parts left out.

The question

1   Read and understand every word of it. If it asks you to compare (the similarities) and/or contrast (the differences) between characters or events, then that is what you must do.

2   Underline all the key words and phrases that mention characters, events and themes, and all instructions as to what to do, e.g. compare, contrast, outline, comment, give an account, write about, show how/what/where.

3   Now write a short list of the things you have to do, one item under the other. A typical question will only have between two and five items at most for you to cope with.

Planning your answer

1   Look at each of the points you have identified from the question. Think about what you are going to say about each. Much of it will be pretty obvious, but if you think of any good ideas, jot them down before you forget them.

2   Decide in what order you are going to deal with the question's major points. Number them in sequence.

3   So far you have done some concentrated, thoughtful reading and written down maybe fifteen to twenty words. You know roughly what you are going to say in response to the question and in what order – if you do not, you have time to give serious thought to trying one of the other questions.

Putting pen to paper

The first sentences are important. Try to summarise your response to the question so the examiner has some idea of how you are going to approach it. Do not say 'I am going to write about the character of Macbeth and show how evil he was' but instead write 'Macbeth was a weak-willed, vicious traitor. Totally dominated by his "fiend-like queen", he deserved the epitaph "this dead butcher" – or did he?' Jump straight into the essay, do not nibble at its extremities for a page and a half. High marks will be gained by the candidate who can show he or she has a mind engaged with the text. Your personal response is rewarded – provided you are answering the question!

As you write your essay *constantly refer back to your list of points* and make sure you are actually responding to them.

How long should it be?

There is no 'correct' length. What you must do is answer the question set, fully and sensitively in the time allowed. Allocate time to each question according to the percentage of marks awarded for it.

How much quotation or paraphrase?

Use only that which is relevant and contributes to the quality and clarity of your answer. Padding is a waste of your time and gains not a single mark.